REACHING OUT

How to
Communicate
Gospel Hope and Love
to
21st Century
Catholics

REACHING OUT

How to
Communicate
Gospel Hope and Love
to
21st Century
Catholics

Joseph Lynch, S.M.

Resurrection Press

An Imprint of
CATHOLIC BOOK PUBLISHING CORP.
Totowa • New Jersey

Dedication

To my father who taught me everything
for living by his deep understanding
and kindness to all people.

‿ೕ౸‿

First published in April 2008 by

    Catholic Book Publishing/Resurrection Press

    77 West End Road

    Totowa, NJ 07512

Copyright © 2008 by Joseph Lynch, S.M.

ISBN 978-1-933066-08-0

Library of Congress Catalog Card Number: 2007940982

Cover design by Geoffrey Butz

Printed in the United States of America

www.catholicbookpublishing.com

Acknowledgments

I HAD been a high school teacher, a counselor and high school chaplain for twenty-five years when Msgr. John Dunne (now Bishop Dunne), director of Priest Personnel in the Diocese of Rockville Centre asked me to be a field resource person in his office. I thank him for the invitation because it necessitated additional education in human resource management and led me into a most rewarding, challenging and useful work.

I owe special thanks to Rudy Vargas IV, director of the Northeast Hispanic Center, a wonderful colleague and friend. He has been a model for me in both understanding group development and in the interpersonal skill required to move an organization. The Spirit has wonderfully gifted him in his valuable work over the years.

Special thanks to another wonderful colleague, advisor and friend, Francois Pierre-Louis, who now teaches political science at Queens College, New York City. Francois has spent much of his life as a field organizer and consultant to grassroots organizations. He has been regional director for PICO, a Jesuit affiliated community-organizing group. Francois was the earliest supporter of putting this book together.

I also owe a special thanks to Jean Nick who as assistant in the Pastoral Planning Office in the diocese of Brooklyn always encouraged me to write no matter how much additional work it meant for her.

Surely I couldn't have survived all the rewrites without the constant help of Anne Kearney who took on so many secretarial chores. Her patience supported my impatience throughout the process. Her quiet responses to some of the things I was saying were invaluable to me. She has a great sense for what opens up worlds to others.

I would also like to express my thanks to Msgr. Bill Hanson and Msgr. Vin Rush of the diocese of Rockville Centre for their persistent and tireless efforts to practice what I describe in these chapters. They have always been sources of hope for me.

I think of the many pastors and leadership people with whom I have worked in recent years in the dioceses of Rockville Centre and Brooklyn, and the archdiocese of New York. They have been an inspiration to me in their commitment to local church life. Their grace, confidence in their people, and humor make them a creative and resilient force.

This book would never have happened without the quiet encouragement of Emilie Cerar who knows quite well how to encourage and support a first effort. She does that so well.

Contents

Foreword

"She may be having some Church questions, but they were not matter for accusation. I just welcomed the accused."

THESE sentences conclude one of the many personal stories told by Joseph Lynch in this book. And here, most fundamentally, is the simple and profound message offered to parish leadership throughout this rich book: *just welcome.* However, the welcoming proposed by Father Lynch as a primary passion and skill of today's parish leadership is not an invitation for them to engage in superficial warm fuzzies that will make everyone briefly feel better. The welcoming described in this book is a challenge to parish leadership to first open our eyes to see who needs to be welcomed, especially the overlooked and the marginalized. Paramount to Father Lynch is a deep concern for young people and those who are baptized but alienated. Then with eyes open, we are further challenged to do the difficult homework that will allow the Gospel of Jesus Christ to transform culture, Church and parish, small group by small group. The serious homework necessary for parish ministry today that is outlined in these pages, asks us to enter the experience of the people we are called to serve, to examine our culture more deeply, and to articulate new language to communicate Gospel hope and love. These efforts to examine and rearticulate will allow us to formulate clear strategic planning in order to *do Church better* in our parishes.

One of my earliest recollections of Joseph Lynch has him sprawled on the floor of his study, because of chronic back pain, reading. He is poised there, glasses askance, surrounded by piles of books; each annotated, underlined and tabbed. His prolific reading was always cross-referenced in an attempt to synthesize the best thinking on a particular topic of interest at any given time. The fruits of Father Lynch's extensive reading

9

and consistent attempts to synthesize are quite evident in these pages and an additional gift to the reader far beyond the particular skills and strategies that are outlined.

Besides sharing his experience as a Marianist religious and priest, teacher, counselor and parish development facilitator, Joseph Lynch provides the parish leader with some of the best contemporary and traditional thinking on the critical topics covered in this book. Father Lynch moves facilely among great minds from Augustine to Merton, to trace outlines, to suggest implications, and to catalogue resources. He grounds his reflections and suggestions in John Paul II's consistent concern that the Church must be about authentic evangelization. Joseph Lynch provides any parish community with a library of resources for reflection and a marvelous tool box with which to begin constructing together a Gospel house in the parish that *just welcomes.* It is the multiplication of these welcoming houses that will help to transform our world and our Church, parish by parish. The founder of the Society of Mary (Marianists), Blessed William Joseph Chaminade, was fond of telling his early followers in the post-Revolution-devastated Church of France, that the renewal of the Church would come from witness and more importantly from the multiplication of witnessing communities. Father Lynch's book is a wonderful contribution to all of us who want to spend our lives in those kinds of witnessing communities and parishes and aren't quite sure where to begin.

Stephen Glodek, S.M.

Introduction

THERE are two things you should know before you begin to read this book. The first is that it is a niche book. It is meant for leadership people in parishes who are engaged in parish councils and committees trying to be effective on the important and large issues of the Church in the United States today. Lay leadership, evangelization, and youth and young adult ministries are just three of those large and important issues that form the core chapters of this book. I purposely use the word "large" because of the vast number of issues that could be discussed within each of those subjects.

The second thing that you will notice is the number of people I rely on to understand these issues. Having been a high-school teacher of religion in the midst of great change in both the United States and the Church, I have had to seek out what critics of culture and the best religious minds were saying. This book is filled with integrating what many good minds think. This integrating task is perhaps the greatest task before us. There has been so much good theological, pastoral and sociological understanding of our faith by scholars that could bring new life to our parishes.

In my early life I thought of myself as an eagle. For the past twenty-five years as a pastoral consultant, I have had to become a mole. I think I am naturally drawn to seeing "the big picture." Working to implement big pictures into the fabric of parish and diocesan programs requires that you come down from the lofty heights and work with the imperfect vision of the mole in less than well-lighted places. I must say it has been a lot of fun establishing processes that lead the Catholic faithful into creative parish and diocesan innovations. Working with two committees that created a truly effective diocesan lay leadership program and with a parish group to establish a well-supported family life program were very satisfying experiences. Dealing with the resistance that parish groups can give to hopeful, imaginative processes can be frustrating at times. Both are part of working in a Spirit-filled but most human church.

You will find a lot of resources mentioned. I would hope that you would investigate further those that seem promising to you. I would go so far as to say that I view this book as a compendium of the best that others have thought and brought to being. (For more extensive listings see the bibliography pp. 147-152.)

My intention is to help you get beyond vague, amorphous discussions and provide you with what I call "entry points" where fruitful discussion that leads to action can begin. You will find two kinds of entry points. The first will be "entry into deeper understanding," the other will be "entry into starting points for action." The best example in my experience to illustrate these was when I was asked by a pastor to work with an evangelization committee that had been meeting monthly for a year. I sat in at my first meeting quietly and listened to discussions about what to do about "fallen away Catholics" and some discussion about welcoming new parishioners. It wasn't a lively discussion and there was a considerable amount of moaning and groaning about "the fallen away." The meeting was characterized by a series of random ideas that followed no particular process. At the second meeting I attended (about their tenth) someone finally said: "Well, what is evangelization anyway?" (They needed "entry into" understanding). No one had ever defined evangelization; no one had ever "framed the question." No one had painted the whole picture. My mole nature activated. Could I paint the large fresco and could we as a group see what the parish had already accomplished? Could we see what still needed to be done; could we choose a part of the fresco that we needed to work on now? You will see in chapter two that I went back to some good work done by Joseph Fichter, S.J. years earlier and to some recent work by Patrick Brennan to start the framing of the evangelization question. Seeing the whole of these "large" issues was all-important before choosing some particular aspect of new parish evangelization efforts.

I am reminded of Daniel Moynihan's dilemma in analyzing the effects of racial inequalities on the black population. He posed the question to himself "where would he begin to work at solutions?" The problems were many: racism, family life, economic problems, education, health, welfare, political power, community issues, religious beliefs and models. After exploring the whole he settled on developing work skills and receiving a living wage as the key to begin to resolve other aspects of racism in America. Such an approach would concentrate the energy of those interested in improving the life of the African American community. It would create pride and independence, restore dignity and self-respect.

I have been using the same methodology of "finding keys" in my work with parishes. I write about three specific issues because I believe that they are the most important and the most difficult to talk about in parishes today. I have worked with parishes on other areas of their concern: e.g., care of the elderly, integration of multiple ethnic groups, affordable housing in gentrifying neighborhoods, family life. The methodology for success is always the same.

1. See the whole—get the framework.
2. See the parts needing attention (strategy).
3. Choose points of entry based on impact (tactics).

4. Become aware of the best thinking and best practices in the Church.

5. Work through all of the above in a systematic planning process.

In order to give more theological depth to what I have to say, I have included a chapter on the pastoral theology of Michael Paul Gallagher, an Irish Jesuit theologian now teaching at the Gregorian University in Rome. His understanding of the Church in the modern situation has been most inspiring and helpful to me.

In addition to the four core chapters I have included two chapters and an appendix that offer new ways of thinking about parish. The first is about "synergy and great groups," a second on planning in a systematic manner. A concluding appendix on "self-managed teams" in the parish, is a reprint of an article originally published in the "Journal of Human Development." We need to imagine structuring such parish development as outlined in that article.

This book is written at the dawn of an age when laity will be primary movers in parish pastoral life. My goal is to help you overcome frustrating discussions and move you on to more open and enthusiastic meetings to realize our potential as Spirit-filled church communities.

1

Lay Leadership

❧

I ENTERED a Catholic religious order, the Society of Mary (Marianists), in 1950. I remember my hope was very specific. I wanted to be a member of a group that was dedicated to fostering the spirituality of what Jesus called "abundant life" to contemporary people. The Marianists, founded by William Joseph Chaminade in the aftermath of the French Revolution, were a response to a decadent Church. The revolution in France against both king and Church was a radical cleansing in the name of "liberty, equality and fraternity." With all its excesses, Chaminade was in sympathy with the deeper aspirations of the Revolution while remaining faithful to the hope of the Gospel and a revivified Church. He recognized very early that it would be the laity who would be the new spring in the Church in France. He began by creating a variety of lay apostolic groups and in their development, religious orders to assist them. The inspiration was certainly a forerunner of the base community movement a century and a half later. I was inspired by his life and work and wanted this to be the focus of my life. Seeing that the religious education of the young had been neglected he also began to open schools. Within 30 years he attracted over 1000 members and had founded over 60 schools.

It was in my early college years that I was privileged to have as mentor Father William Ferree. He was a man of great breadth and originality of mind and had done his doctoral work in the social justice teaching of Pius XI. During his tenure as director of our college program he gave us weekly conferences around the themes of lay leadership, lay spirituality and the social virtues, (a field still almost totally unknown). I grew up with the sense that "the reform of the institutions" (as Pius XI called it) was the work of our time in the Church.

In *Quadragesimo Anno,* Pius XI had laid the groundwork. In a well-known passage he said: "the good intentions of individuals are no longer enough. It is institutions that need reform." Popes from Leo XIII on had seen clearly that the "structured disorder" of economic and political life were causing immense social evils. Capital and labor were the recurrent themes of the early papal encyclicals of the century. Later popes would be concerned about international relationships, family life, racism, world poverty and peace. I received my early orientation on the role of the laity in the modern world in this milieu. It was a spirituality orientated towards the needs of the social order.

As Western society grew more affluent through the fifties, I saw a new set of issues arise. We were an "image culture": a "psychology of affluence" had begun what Daniel Yankelovich, a noted critic, labeled "expressive individualism." It was marked by sharp discontinuities from traditional life-styles. The late 1940s and 50s had seen society recovering economically and had been marked by middle-class social conformity. As Yankelovich points out, protests on campus were less about radical politics than about cultural value shifts. "We lurched from puritanical repressive attitudes about sexuality to open unrepressed sexuality, from duty to pleasure, from saving to spending." In the 1970s the new values were held by only 3% of the population. By 1980, a formidable 80% of the population accepted at least part of the new value orientation. "It all added up to a radical extension of individualism." There is just no doubt that the 60s marked a values revolution. We, as Church, have experienced the revolution but have not understood or coped with it well.

The 1st century world was certainly not an easy world to evangelize but the first Christians knew the Gospel's power to integrate the best of culture and prevail over what was unworthy of human life and so when I think of lay leadership in our parishes today I imagine that we can create a group of highly aware and enlightened parishioners who can create processes that challenge what Robert Bly, the poet and social critic calls "the giants" of our culture ("the principalities of powers" of our day).

Lay Formation or Lay Leadership?

Understanding the cultural forces that have created changed consciousness in our people is most important for us. We need to know who we are as Catholic Christians today but we need to know the forces that are affecting the people of our time. We will return to the consciousness theme in the next two chapters. The "lay formation" mentality seems to concentrate very much on a kind of traditional "Catholic updating" curriculum. I don't doubt that many of those who seek more education for ministry need such an updating. However, without a critical cultural component just described and without much more leadership skill training, we will not have prepared people well enough for taking an active role in the contemporary Church.

I have sat through diocesesan planning sessions for "lay formation programs" and have heard such discussions as: "Will they find ministry back in the parish when they finish the program?" "What are we forming for?" The real questions for lay people today should be: "What do I want to do?" "What am I called to do?" and "What do I need to learn?" The first set of questions comes from a sort of "warehouse" mentality of lay apostolate. Give the people a general background, update them in basic theology, and *hope* they find a niche in the parish. In the second set of questions more effort is spent on personal discernment, the social justice issues of the world and neighborhood, and in the skills required to meet the discipleship needs of today.

The active spirit of lay leadership I am talking about has been described very well by Msgr. Frank Schneider, former Chancellor of the Diocese of Rockville Centre, in a talk entitled "The Rights of Co-Ministers in the Church." These rights are listed in canons 208-221 as "the baptismal rights of the Christian faithful."

They are:

1. The right to cooperate (canon 208)
2. The right to evangelize (canon 211)
3. The right to petition and make known needs (canon 212)
4. The right to recommend (canon 212)
5. The right to receive the word of God and the Sacraments (canon 213)
6. The right to follow one's proper spirituality (canon 214)
7. The right to promote the apostolate and one's proper initiative in apostolic work (canon 216)
8. The right to a Christian education (canon 217)
9. The right to academic freedom (canon 218)
10. The right to vindicate one's rights in a Church court (canon 221)
11. The right to be judged fairly if summoned to judgment by competent authority (canon 221)
12. The right to legality in regard to church penalties (canon 221)

It is worthy of note that canon law uses the strong language of rights. It could have used softer language such as "cooperate with diocesan planning in evangelization" or "cooperating with pastors and their staffs." No, this is stronger language. Lay people have the *right* to cooperate, the *right* to evangelize, the *right* to one's proper spirituality. There is recognition of the strength and gifts of Christian adults presupposed in this language. It is not language for the dependent or the immature. The language canon law uses founds the confidence with which we need to imagine our people when we speak of programs for the laity. The "right to promote the apostolate and one's proper initiative as apostolic work" is not the same as recruiting three volunteers for the food pantry. Respect for unique gifts, the presence of the Holy Spirit, wise discernment, creativity and proactive individuals are all implied in this co-ministry understanding.

We find the same spirit of profound respect for the lay vocation in recent Church documents. *The Decree of the Apostolate of the Laity* tells us that:

> The laity derives the right and duty to the apostolate from their union with Christ the Head . . . *they are assigned to the apostolate by the Lord Himself. The laity are not parish volunteers, they are persons called and sent by Christ.* Laywomen and men need to be nourished and strengthened in their own calling and identity (National Council of Catholic Bishops, "Our Hearts Were Burning Within Us").

The American bishops have said, "Adult catechesis must be regarded as a preferential option in planning programming . . . such lifelong formation must be considered the *chief form of catechesis.*" Understanding what this means in the light of adult learners is the task of the later part of this chapter.

John Paul II indicated to priests that they make sure: "That all of the faithful shall be led in the Holy Spirit to the full devel-

opment of his or her vocation through the Gospel teaching . . .
the ministerial priesthood is at the service of the common priesthood
and directed at the unfolding of the Baptismal grace of all
Christians."

These statements are quite a charter for both laity and clergy and need to root and ground us in our search to be faithful
to the lay vocation. My experience teaches me that at least 20 to
30% of parishioners want to be involved in this kind of understanding and discernment of their life experience. In one very
active parish I was engaged as a consultant because *only* 70% of
the Sunday Mass population was "active" in ministry. Ministry
here was very orientated toward excellent liturgy, building
community and serving neighborhood social needs.

Cecelia Alison Hahn and Loren Mead of the Alban Institute,
an ecumenical consulting group, have both written thoughtful
articles on parishioners' discovery of themselves and their
calls. Hahn says that "transformational learning happens when
the depth of my life—my yearnings, my shaky places, my
deepest joys, my fears and my failures connect with the symbols and story of my church and tradition. When these two stories meet, Gospel may happen."

Mead's article goes on to describe a new paradigm for
parish life. This change calls people from "support" to "active
engagement." It is comparable to the move from "being an
annual subscriber to the symphony to realizing that you and
your friends have to pick up the oboes and bassoons and vio-
lins and make music . . . If there is going to be music, you have
to make it." That description written in 1990 should be clear for
us now as we undergo a vast decline in priests and religious in
our time in North America. Catholic people cannot be specta-
tors at the symphony any longer. However, Mead warns us
that our people have two reservations about this new role.

1. They are not universally enthusiastic about this new responsibility.
2. They are often afraid. They are not clear what they are to be and do.

In all Christian churches the predominant model of ministry, inherited from Europe had been the clergy, now the primary model has to be the laity. So Mead calls for a new structure: "the reinvented congregation." Congregations need to become life-long centers of ministry and ministry development. In Mead's model there are two catecumenates. The first is called "the catecumenate of membership" which includes all sacramental preparations whose aim would be to bring people out of an ambiguous culture into discipleship and an apostolic community. The second parish catecumenate sends people to the world and receives them back for reflection. Education at this point would be relevant to the world being faced by the member. For example, issues that deal with economics in a Christian light, the challenges of the workplace, violence in society, poverty, immigration and an examination of neighborhood issues would be subjects for reflection. Some system of field education would be necessary to process learnings taking place. Mentoring would be necessary. This is classical theological reflection. Mead at this point warns us that "training laity in schools or methods of clergy theology may be counterproductive. It's more likely to turn out second-rate clergy type theology, and worse convince laity to go to seminary to get the "real thing." In this model the parish is a place of reflection, "the village oasis" of John Paul II.

Laity in this time of reflection need to examine their lives, discern and raise questions about their Christian discipleship. Mead concludes, "Most of us (clergy) do not know how to do any of this." We didn't buy this when we signed up and many do not want the role. I suspect that many core parishioners would be ready to "reinvent the congregation" in this way; I also suspect it is where many of the young would be attracted. Oddly enough, I know a number of parish-based "moms and tots" groups that have been doing just as Mead describes. In this kind of cultural discernment topics such as money, work, leisure-time activities, television's influence on the family and the war in Iraq have surfaced among these young mothers.

Sherry Wedell's Distinctions As Entry Points

As I said in the introduction of the book my hope is to take large issues like lay leadership and find points of entry where you might most usefully begin discussion. Another useful model for those of you involved in developing lay leadership programs is to consider framing the question in the categories of Sherry Wedell of the Catherine of Siena Institute in her monograph *Making Disciples, Equipping Apostles*. The distinction she makes among adult faith formation, gift discernment and lay leadership training is one such useful entry point distinction.

1. **Adult Faith Formation** is education in the body of knowledge essential to living a full Christian life. It is what Loren Mead call the "first catechumenate." Discipleship is the goal in raising the consciousness of Christian teaching. Classic examples of content in diocesan adult faith formation programs seem to center around: introduction to Old and New Testament ecclesiology, theology of ministry, liturgy and sacraments, and morality. I have seen two weaknesses in this part of the program. First, it tends to be the whole program of lay ministry preparation. As I said earlier it often looks a lot

like "Catholic updating." The content needs to be more focused on the Church's mission in the world today, and on the lay vocation and discipleship.

2. **Gift Discernment** is seen by Wedell as the single most important critical personal skill. For any person it is about the particular individual's gifts and as such would provide the most wonderful "entry point" in ministry education. I have seen people come to wonder, appreciation and even astonishment at gift discernment workshops. It will be the way the laity connects to the whole Church and is the essence of lay leadership for the individual. Most often it is not given anywhere near sufficient attention in lay leadership programs. For Weddell gift discernment includes the following discernments:

- The talents and spiritual gifts (charisms) given by God
- The personal call or vocation
- The lead of the Holy Spirit in one's life
- The meaning and value of your world and time
- The creative application of church teaching in your specific situations, e.g. in law, nursing, medicine, teaching, engineering, business.

At the end of this chapter, I will say more about gift discernment methodologies.

3. **Lay Leadership Skills** include equipping leaders in the Pauline understanding of enabling disciples to help others minister. Wedell's model imagines that only with layers of leadership can every member of the Church receive adequate attention. These skills are orientated toward action. Some typical examples include:

- Communication skills, especially skills at listening
- Group process skills, especially consensus building

- Leadership skills
- Facilitation of small group skills
- Systematic planning skills
- Conflict management skills
- Organizing and delegating skills
- Mentoring and coaching skills

Parish groups reflecting on lay leadership can choose entry points to begin or continue work in leadership. Many of the skills listed above may be available at local colleges in the social work or business schools. The best program I have found has been at the National Training Laboratories Institute (N.T.L.), whose catalogue could amaze you with the relevance of its curriculum for leadership training. The Alban Institute, an ecumenical training institute also has some very helpful programs. We need to become familiar with the possibilities offered in such training. It is so important for church leadership at every level to know and be able to utilize these skills. We are extremely lacking at the present time.

We are at the point in most dioceses where .01 percent of all Catholics are clergy and religious. It is important to stare at that figure for a while: 99.9% of Catholics are lay Catholics. Only about 1% of priests prior to the Council of Trent received the kind of formal education that we consider normative today. We consider it a tragedy if our children drop out of school at the age of sixteen. We know that they are not prepared for adult life in America. Why do we still not consider the termination of religious education at the time of Confirmation a tragic occurrence? Ongoing religious education is a necessity in our culture. We say we believe that the Holy Spirit has given particular gifts and vocations to all. Weddell is quite clear: "pastors and pastoral leaders need to be formed themselves to form adults. This formation will require a great effort but it is worth the price for it provides a remedy that will clear our minds and open hearts to realities we could not have guessed." Pope John Paul II expressed the same hope in a talk to French Bishops in 1982: "On the practical level it is also important to bring more imagination and daring to the concept of the possible areas of participation by the laity, since those are far from being fully explored."

Addendum: On Gift Discernment

About thirty years ago I attended a 3-hour-gift discernment workshop conducted by Loughlan Sofield at a gift discernment workshop. As part of a very simple exercise we were asked to make a list of the gifts we thought we might have. I think my list numbered about fifteen. I have updated that list over the years and have added to it at subsequent gift workshops. I now number about forty distinctive characteristics that I call gifts. As my realization grew over the years, the more I realized the truth of Paul's words "what are you that you have not received." Realization of gifts brings humility. In 1985 I attended a workshop sponsored by the Alban Institute on "Volunteering in the Church." The title was slightly deceptive. It was a five-day workshop on methodologies for discerning gifts in congregations. Activities like sentence completions, use of the T.A.T. (Thematic Apperception Test) and interviewing methodologies were among the subjects of the week. It became clear to me that Catholic parishes generally start with the needs in their community, and request volunteers to fill those needs. The hope is that generous people will respond. The Alban approach was not based on searching for "volunteers" but was built on members searching within themselves for the particular gifts that the Spirit had given. It was not based on immediate needs for volunteers as much as a long-term plan to engage all the members of the Church in particular ministries to which they were "called." When I returned from Alban I put my large folder of material in the back of my closet. I liked the discernment of gifts approach but I felt that Catholic parishes would find this approach too alien and too long-range.

In later years I found the Network Ministries International materials and used it at workshops I have led in Catholic parishes. It is used at Pastor Bill Hybel's Willow Creek Church in Illinois where the congregation is above 10,000. The Network materials have been very helpful. Its basic approach is built around two inventories: a passion questionnaire of nine questions that locates energy around particular interests and a 133-item questionnaire around "spiritual gifts." This process leads to discerning among twenty-three gifts mentioned in the Epistles of St. Paul. There is a modified Catholic version of the spiritual gift questionnaire developed by Father Nicholas Figlioli that has been published by Network. Fr. Figlioli had revised some of the language to make it more "Catholic."

The diocese of Rockville Centre, where I worked for some years, has developed materials for a weekend workshop as part of its pastoral leadership program, "Discovering Your Spiritual Gifts." They also engaged Jean Morris Trumbauer to assist parishes who wished to do gift discernment solely through the interviewing process. (Jean Morris Trumbauer, *A Practical Guide for Transforming Volunteering in Ministry*, "Sharing the Ministry," Augsburg Fortress).

Any interviewing process will involve parish commitment. It would mean training a corps of interviewers. I have done this in a few parishes and think it is feasible for those parishes that are highly committed to developing lay leadership.

Two years ago I was asked to assist an African American parish of about 400 members in a gift discernment process for their leadership people (about fifty). Here the people knew each other so well I simply adopted the Sofield process described above. They made a list of what they thought were their individual gifts. They then shared their lists in small groups. The group was very affirming in recognizing gifts mentioned as well as pointing out additional gifts that they could discern among their members.

Somewhat later I discovered the work of the Catherine of Siena Institute, a Catholic group that offers workshops around the country based on *Catholic Spiritual Gifts Inventory*, by Sherry Weddell and a workbook entitled "Discerning Charisms" by Weddell & Huntington. Father Figlioli who has surveyed gift discernment material in the United States considers the Catherine of Siena processes the most thoughtful. I have some reservations because of the fewer number of items in their questionnaire and the fewer categories than the Network instrument.

Finally, the Gallup organization has developed an on-line instrument available to parishes for a nominal fee called "Strength Finders." Although I liked the instrument very much, I have two hesitations: it is more suited for an educated clientele and the categories of gift areas do not use familiar Christian terminology. Some translation into more traditional Catholic categories may be needed at the local level.

If you are interested in pursuing an ongoing parish gift discernment program it may be worthwhile to establish an ad hoc committee to look into the above approaches and material. At the end of this addendum I have provided the addresses of all the above sources.

In conclusion, some groups have begun using the Enneagram or Meyers-Briggs Type Inventory to begin a process in the parish. Local presenters are usually available. *Life*

Keys, (Bethany Press, Minneapolis) authored by Jane Kise, David Stark and Sandra Krebs Hirsch is a correlation of Meyers-Briggs to the search for life gifts, passions and spiritual gifts.

Some concluding notes on gifts:

1. John Haughey, S.J. notes that our gifts tend to be integrated within each of us. That became clear to me when I realized that my sixth ranked gift in the Network instrument "shepherding" was really the motivation for wanting to develop other gifts on which I scored higher: discernment, wisdom, teaching, mercy, encouragement.

2. Karl Rahner, S.J. puts it powerfully when he says "that the charismatic element is the first and most ultimate among the formal characteristics inherent in the very nature of the Church as such. The institutional factor in the Church remains encompassed by the charismatic movement of the Spirit in the Church. The giftedness of each member is the base on which the institutional effectiveness of the Church is built."

3. Doris Donnelly in the introduction to *Retrieving Charisms for the Twenty-First Century* describes three surprises about charisms:

   a. Charisms emerge *everywhere* in the Church and in the world. The gifts of the Holy Spirit are not confined to ecclesial institutions or to ecclesially affiliated people but emerge in all those who do anything well for the good of others.

   b. Charisms may be found wherever there are human needs. Jesus promised to be with us and so when human needs are neglected and evil seems to reign what we have to do is "look harder" to find the charism needed. They are the "invisible gifts" needed to be made manifest for the needs of the body. That is the exciting challenge awaiting all of us in leadership positions in the Church. This is the delight of the Spirit working in people.

c. Most of God's graces are given for the sake of those receiving them but charisms are the unique gifts given for the common good. It is of their very nature that gifts are not private possessions. They are God's way of building families, parishes, businesses, communities, cities, and the Church.

4. In the same book, John Haughey, S.J. in a most insightful article, "Christians, an Ecclesiological Exploration" describes charisms, as "enabling many people to do ordinary things extraordinarily well." Occasionally, charisms enable a few people to do extraordinary things. If we think of them only in this latter sense we miss the frequency and richness around us.

Haughey sees our gifts as ordinarily following human growth patterns. We naturally pay attention to what we desire. We grow in certain directions. In all, there is an underlying desire in Christians to grow into something "the birds in the air can find strength in." "Without the desire to be for others gifts will never mature." So, to you, reader, who are in this path we celebrate the journey in whatever place you serve the Body. Haughey concludes that without the gifts of the people the Church easily becomes "monotonous," "uniform" and "lifeless." They enliven both the inner life of the Church and enrich the institution making it a more vital community.

2

The Pastoral Theology of
Michael Paul Gallagher, S.J.

⚬⌒⌒⚬

WHILE I was doing a preliminary draft of this book I realized that it needed some deeper theology than I had been sketching. This book was meant to be practically helpful to parish staffs and councils but I found I was not happy with its "practicality." A theology had been forming within me all of my life. Family experiences, early Church memories, Catholic school religious education, courses in philosophy and theology, seminary studies based on the works of Thomas Aquinas, a master's degree in Religious Education and experiences in teaching religion and literature as well as being a counselor of high school students and adults had been working its synthesis in me. I know I had an "operational theology" working but like most people I had made no systematic formulations. In wrestling with this problem of not being articulate about my underlying beliefs I remembered liking the first book I had read of Michael Paul Gallagher, *Clashing Symbols*. Upon re-reading it I decided to go back and read some of his other writings. It was most fortuitous; we were kindred spirits sharing similar journeys and similar approaches to people. I have decided to preface the next two chapters with one on the pastoral theology of Michael Paul Gallagher to communicate the spirit underlying the practical advice I offer.

Gallagher, an Irish Jesuit, was a professor of literature of the University College in Dublin for twenty years before he was invited to Rome as a member of the Pontifical Council for Culture. He now teaches fundamental theology at the

Gregorian University. His work with young people in Dublin had led him deeply into the problems of indifference and unbelief. The massive religious change that had taken place in Ireland among the young during those years certainly prepared him to understand the religious changes of our time. His work as a member of the Pontifical Institute of Culture made him aware of the best contemporary efforts to understand the modern problem of faith. What follows will be largely verbatim, with some paraphrasing and reordering of his thought to make it more cogent for my purpose. While I will suggest some "entry points" of my own in the next two chapters, this chapter will offer many theological frames of reference and processes for reflection before plunging into action. I also hope Michael Paul Gallagher becomes more well known in North America. I believe he speaks to the needs we have more than anyone I know.

Overcoming Childhood Images of God

In *The Human Poetry of Faith* Gallagher quotes a character in an Aidan Matthew's short story:

"I believe that we are adored by the living mystery we dare to call God. I believe that God invites us to take His dear cherishing of us at His word and to live always and everywhere in the spirit of it, giving and forgiving along the way so as to divine at last our own human nature. I believe this word of pledge and promise from God in the word that we are loveable —loved—to be spoken and broken most bountifully in the life and death and real presence of Jesus of Nazareth, that this person is the high point of God's love for us.

"In the Gospel Jesus liberates God and us from the sub-Christian pictures that inhabit our imagination. Jesus evangelizes God so to speak, because the only God worth believing in meets us in unexpected ways in Jesus. Jesus is not the God of power but of Presence, not of Distant Majesty but Passionate Artistry, like a love-sculptor carving love shapes out of resisting stone . . . not aloof from the human chaos but the shocking figure recognized by the centurion at the cross: 'truly this man was the Son of God.' Meeting the Jesus of the Gospels will entail leaving behind the always-lingering immaturity of our God images. Karl Rahner asks the question 'is sovereignty the essential characteristic of God—or is it the capacity for relationship . . . Only if we understand our being needed by God do we really learn to think in a liberating way. St. Paul expressed it with such simplicity: 'He loved me and gave himself up for me' " (Gal. 2:20).

These citations represent Gallagher's spirit as he approaches the issues of faith today. He quotes Paul VI who spoke of approaching even atheists of our time with "immense sympathy." God is not the "retired architect" of the universe or the "distant enemy" of our freedom—the power "up there."

The crucial point is that so many people try to survive on childhood images of God and so they court immaturity of faith. People today seldom lose faith by conscious rejection but rather by their images of God ceasing to inform their experience. Quoting a delegate to an annual meeting of priests in Ireland he compares the Church to a ship letting in water from below the surface; the captain and crew know that there are leaks but they prefer not to examine them too closely. Another version of this is to imagine the Church as an old car, coughing a lot but chugging along; the driver avoids bringing it to a garage for a check-up for fears that something even worse could be diagnosed. Or again, it may be compared to a man hearing noises downstairs during the night; if he lies in bed too

long merely wondering what could have fallen, the burglar
may have come and gone by the time he decides to go downstairs. What these three parables have in common is the recognition that non-recognition of the new faith situation is a real
danger. It is necessary to explain why a new context of faith has
developed. If we are in search of a theology of non-panic, it will
be necessary to have a clear grasp of the roots and causes of the
present influences on religion.

Gallagher describes three groups of young people. The first
group has had the bottom fall out of whatever faith and practice they may have inherited, and the result is that within the
space of a few years the whole world of religion has come to
mean very little to them. He thinks of them as victims of a kind
of cultural injustice, meaning that newer life-styles have
robbed them of their roots and kidnapped their consciousness
in different directions. Family, Church and school proved inadequate to help them find genuine faith for today. The second
group is those who are fortunate to have found some new
focus for their faith. Very often they do this through belonging
to some small community of people who are working towards
some level of Christian commitment. They are the seekers and
finders of the Gospel. The third group he calls the "in-
betweens." They continue to "practice," perhaps with less reg-
ularity than their parents would hope, but they have not opted
out of the Church. Neither have they opted into any Christian
commitment. They are in an undernourished limbo. They hang
on to what their parents hang on to, but they are not their parents and so what gave nourishment to their parents' faith can
fail to feed their younger lives. They have inherited a rich
tradition, but they seldom experience its richness. The key
question is how they may make the move from conventional
religion to a religion of personal conviction. As John Cardinal

Newman said, "mere inherited faith in those who can have an intelligent faith is, to say the least, dangerous and inconsistent." Years ago Karl Rahner wrote that faith itself has not changed in our time but the world around it has changed drastically. Faith today has to be a decision and will not easily be a "smooth fitting into the tradition of parents." Those were the days when belonging to a Church and following its practices seemed identical to "faith." People inherited a whole way of life and usually stayed within it.

"The religious crisis of recent years seems to be one of indifference on a larger scale and a falling away from the practice of faith by previous believers." Gallagher had followed the extensive research in French Canada on the decline of religious practice. This research had seriously questioned the optimistic hypothesis that faith can often continue in individuals despite a decline in religious practice. The progression from initial to fuller indifference is relatively easy to follow.

Degrees of "Distancing" Among Baptized Catholics

Certainly, the research indicates that the abandonment of Mass-going is not to be dismissed lightly. The loss of community support for faith, the absence of the pedagogy of the Word and sacraments are notable losses for the life of faith. Andre Carron, in Montreal, a student of contemporary atheism in France and French Canada has differentiated eight "distancing" patterns among baptized Catholics. The eight patterns are:

1. Abandonment of regular attendance at Mass and the sacraments.
2. Alienation from the institutional Church: this can be active or passive depending on whether a person had definite objection to the Church or is simply drifting with secularized society.

3. Non-belonging with the Church as a community; again some will be more passive and remain nominal Catholics, whereas others will cut their links more consciously, even angrily.

4. Fading of Christian values in practice, where there is no longer any real impact of belief on behavior.

6. Collapse of the credibility of the Christian meaning for life involving some rejection of Church teaching, or of the Gospel itself.

6. Withdrawal of belonging in faith to Jesus Christ. This is the point where one arrives at unbelief in the strict sense.

7. Rejection of a personal God, either agnostic suspension of judgment, or atheistic denial of God's existence.

8. Apathy over all religious questions. At this point there is a complete absence of interest in the possibility of faith.

Gallagher comments that the immediate danger to faith is not unbelief but shallow belief. Sunday practice may no longer lead to strong faith. Many new forms of support activities are required if we are to avoid Christian malnutrition in today's world. Consumer economics can quietly replace religion—something that both Marx and Freud foresaw. To remain on the level of individualist piety rather than social concern, or on the level of convention rather than conviction means we would not survive as a strong Church in a more secular environment.

The young particularly can be turned off by organized religion as it has been experienced by them. They can be equally and painfully adrift from the assumptions and values of parents and teachers. Gallagher offers two major insights about these phenomena. Firstly, that it is still more accurate to speak of a communication gap rather than a generation gap. Secondly, that Catholics in Ireland seem to be over-sacramentalized and under-evangelized. These two comments are worthy of reflection and discussion in the American Catholic Church today. From Carron's stages we might observe that most "non-practicing" American Catholics fall into his first two stages. We can easily imagine further drift into stages three and four over time.

Carron sees the causes of unbelief today as the convergence of four factors. It is a story of two dramatically new forces meeting with two fairly unchanging conservative factors. On one hand we have the emergence of radically new ways of living, accompanied by a whole new cluster of ideas and attitudes. On the other hand we have a Church cautious and slow to move and families and individuals unready for the business of finding their bearings in this new world. One has only to recall family life before television to have an idea of the significant change in most people's experience of home. Add mobility and the entertainment industry that finds a ready market for a family with disposable income to be spent on children. What emerges is the uprooting of many traditional ways of relating in the family and the dominance of a new culture. The dangers of a consumer society driving out the sense of mystery in the young is all too obvious. Walter Kasper, German theologian and Cardinal, even finds that indifference to belief in God is by far the most plausible attitude to take. Christ Himself describes the choking of the good seed among thorns—the distractions of superficial living playing a major part. Distractions keep people from boredom but also from finding the deeper truths of their life. T.S. Eliot described it as "distracted from distraction by distraction." The entertainment and consumer-driven society keeps mystery at a distance and aborts religious questions. "It provides alternative sacralizations—sex, sports, security, success." Gallagher sees that rapid social change spells the death of conventional religion in so far as it remains conventional. Chapter four, on youth, will explore this at greater length.

Discovering God in Human Life

After Vatican II the German Jesuit theologian, Karl Rahner had seen that the Church had shifted the agenda of faith away from the traditional emphasis on explicit beliefs, Church mediations, and conceptual creeds and even from scriptural revelation as central and foundational. He chose to search for God more slowly, more tentatively—starting from human mystery as the gateway to divine mystery. In Rahner's theology, God is always present at the center of each human life. He is less interested in what believers or unbelievers think or say than in the realm of encounter with mystery happening at the heart of each existence. A unique story is unfolded in each person. This pastoral shift Rahner calls "mystagogy," and it invokes a dialogue of discernment around the calls of life where freedom and grace meet.

People today need to make Christian faith more real through exploring their ordinary but deep experiences. There is this hidden poetry in people. We live with unvisited spaces in ourselves. It is hard to find the key on one's own and most often requires someone who is listening and present to us. Listening is necessary to get to what Shakespeare called "the melting mood." When doors of imagination open to something of self-tenderness, we become ready for God. God's Spirit is at work in all that is good in us. Our crucial hungers are more human than explicitly religious. We need to "start further back" before jumping into doctrinal language too early; we need to pay attention to the soil of experience into which the

Sower is sowing today. We can risk putting the cart before the horse. The Bible communicates on a non-doctrinal level—that of story, of experience of slow discovery. At its simplest it wants to evoke human experiences of depth and to ponder them as the theater of the Spirit. It hopes to show that these encounter points with God are more frequent than we think. There is a larger drama of growth that is lived out in different ways in everyone. Many people have encountered the Christian vision only in tired language and frozen forms. The hope that we have is to awaken the sleeping beauty of our wonder about ourselves so that we can be ready for the greater wonder that is Jesus Christ. Quoting Douglas Copeland's, *Girlfriend In a Coma:* "There must be all these people everywhere on earth, so desperate for just the smallest sign that there is something finer or larger or more miraculous about ourselves than we had supposed. How can I give them a spark?"

Faith takes many forms, not just the official ones. We need spirituality for those who are frequently put off by Church language and who feel themselves disappointed and undernourished by their surrounding culture. How do we see ourselves? What do we hope for? What is it all about? The deeper answers are found in how we imagine our lives. It is at that level that we find either anchors of wisdom or suffer from dispersion and emptiness. The failure of conventional religion is that it does not tap the spiritual roots of our journeying. It assumes that everyone can hear and understand the scriptures or enter the wavelength of the liturgy without difficulty. Instead, many people are nowhere near the threshold of such readiness. They are untouched by ceremonies that were forged for another culture. They are in need of a more sensitive initiation to their own spiritual drama. We need to do justice to their human hungers. Gallagher continues: "Our hearts are always on the look-out for vision, love, fullness, surprise—if only we can emerge from the prison of our smaller concerns. Within ordinary human experience are untapped sources of wonder. Within easy reach of anyone is a different way of seeing things." His pastoral credo has emerged over the years: people are hungry for a different space of self-hearing and self-healing and when they find it they spontaneously start looking for God. This space is born from honesty and from the presence of another person who is not afraid of a slow journey through the desert. Gallagher concludes: "There is a Christian reading of the narratives of our lives. At these paradox thresholds the spirit is creative, waiting to write a divine story, even before we know it is divine. Everyone is being saved—secretly as it were whenever there is a birthplace of 'yes' in one's life. To use biblical analogies, our human Passovers are both preparations for grace and places of grace. The adventure of Exodus happens in experiences such as friendship or humility or solidarity or solitude, or in the calls of the everyday."

In an imaginary dialogue between Jane Austen and D.H.Lawrence, Gallagher puts it this way:

DHL: The long adventure of tenderness is where most people emerge from their fears. I look on it as a lifelong space of healing.

JA: Surely the threshold is to face the full range of who we are and to face it with the loved friend.

John Henry Newman, as an Anglican, preached an unusual sermon around Christmas in which he spoke of avoidance of our human "wounds" as the reason why our religious beliefs remain so unreal. Newman saw this fear of facing our shadows as the root of our shallowness.

In commenting on Bernanos' *Diary Of a Country Priest*, Gallagher quotes the unnamed curate as saying: "God wants us to be merciful with ourselves." All the great religious words have meaning in us: forgiveness, humility, faith, hope, love, peace . . . But without some human journey into honesty often religious life will lack roots and staying power. If we are not in touch with these deep essentials, we lack human starting points for religious faith. The rhythms of our culture can keep us disconnected from ourselves hence disconnected from God. As Von Hugel, the English writer on the mystical life says: "It is through ordinary non-religious moments that imperceptible grace finds material to work in and on very much. God loves the average very much in the poor little virtue, the poor little insight."

People are not hostile to the truth at the core of the Gospel but they are often unreachable by the usual church language. Sebastian Moore has remarked that the "ineffectiveness of organized religion today is due to its failure to speak to the pre-religious God awareness." From neglect of the mysteries within, to a trivialized and pragmatic culture, we are starving ourselves. Thomas Merton says it well: "people are in every way prevented from getting inside themselves. Our greatest problem is lack of depth. Newman speaks to the contemporary situation when he says: 'if we make light of what is deepest in us. . . . 'to seem' becomes 'to be.' "

What does the pre-religious dimension imply? Most of all that we have an inner core of Spirit-guided desire before we arrive at explicitly Christian interpretations of our experience. Gallagher summarizes: "Our hearts are being drawn towards love prior to finding the face of love in Christ. Then there is a risk of rushing into the world of explicit religion without pausing on what is more fundamental in each of us—the experience of searching, or struggling to live genuinely, of being slowly transformed by the adventure of life. Only with reverence for the natural pace of people's searching can the Gospel be heard with new power and the only lasting faith for today will be born from a free decision. Finally, without some personal relationship with Christ, nothing will last in religion today. And you have to choose to make that happen in some way, through some gateway that suits you. Best to do it as Aquinas tells us: St. Augustine says: 'make humanity your way and you shall arrive at God. It is better to limp along that way then to stride along some other route.' "

What the Church Has to Do

Gallagher has some strong words for church leaders: "to continue to spend too much energy in serving the conventional needs of the conventional believer is hardly obedient to the Lord's precept: leave the majority of ninety-nine in the desert and seek out, caringly and creatively, even a minority of one. . . . In other words a church that seems indifferent to those who begin to feel indifferent can only confirm their indifference. For modern people living with a self-sufficient, pragmatic and technological mindset, religion can seem unnecessary. As Saul Bellow the American novelist puts it, 'The world is too much with us and there never has been so much world.' " It is so easy not to pay attention.

Gallagher indicates three specifics that have allowed the alienation from faith to take place: The teaching of religion in schools, failings in the pastoral ministry of the Church, and weakness in the quality of Christian living in families and society. He accepts the fact that the Church is accused of the "externalist" heresy—putting so much emphasis in external conformism and neglecting the personal assimilation of religion necessary for our time. Even the document of the Second

Vatican Council "Church in the Modern World" admits that: "believers can have more than a little to do with the birth of atheism." Yves Congar, the French Dominican theologian, looks on modern atheism and indifference less as a shutting out of God than a rejection of how God has been presented. "In much unbelief today it is what we have done with religion rather than God that is being rejected."

Gallagher places most emphasis for the faith of the next generation on the family: "Now that the tide has changed, the family is the main place to learn to survive against the tide; to keep that metaphor, the school and the Church can usually only improve on the basic skill of swimming learned in the family. If this picture is correct, it means that malnutrition or mediocrity of faith within the family can cause a silent, but sinister erosion of faith in the next generation."

The danger for children of the future is not that they will have little or poor contact with the Church, but that they will live on the surface of themselves and never experience the hungers of the heart, questions of mind, or spaces of the spirit that could put them in touch with their real selves. They could live with so much dull prose that they never find their own poetry.

In the conversion experience we must hope for today, less emphasis will be on "continuity of practice" than preparing for more explicit commitment of faith. Up to now much teaching and preaching seemed to assume that continuity of practice was possible and sufficient. It has not been sufficient and in our new situation it may not be possible either, unless rooted in some adult conversion. Many can lose personal faith because they have lost confidence in the institution. Gallagher frequently returns to three forms of lapsing from faith: apathy, alienation and anger. Apathy is a "form of socio-cultural loss of faith: it is largely passive. It stems from this new environment and results in a dull indifference to the spiritual dimension of life. It is a drifting with the social tide, with the secular environment that is uninterested rather than hostile towards faith. "To allow oneself to be kidnapped by the consumerist way of life, the bourgeois paradise, leads ultimately to an untroubled, unconscious, even casual abandoning of the Christian faith. As St. Paul put it to Timothy: 'they will keep the outer forms of religion but will reject its inner power' " (2 Tim 3:5).

In another place Gallagher sees the journey out of apathy arising from an awakening of hope, a positive experience within the self. Alienation by comparison with apathy is more agitated and troubled. It is less a drifting than a disappointment with institutional life within the Church. A theology of unbelief must include an ecclesiological chapter because the human face of the Church can be a counter-witness and a source of unbelief. Forms of worship, which are "boring," "irrelevant," "annoying," "more a nuisance than a help" are cited often by the young. Precise sources of dissatisfaction with conventional religion and priests and religious who are seen as embodiments of this conventionality come in for harsh evaluation. It would seem that this kind of alienation could only be met by the many forms of small group renewal in the Church today.

The third term Gallagher uses to describe loss of faith is "anger." Apathy is a danger for a large number of people. Alienation affects the more searching and better educated. Anger seems to affect a small but important fringe. Some of those who are "angry" have intellectual reasons for rejecting; others tend to be more socio-political, i.e. angry with a religion of mere piety or mere obligation. Paul VI in his encyclical *Ecclesiam Suam* spoke of this group as "sometimes men of great breath of mind, impatient with mediocrity and self-seeking."

Gallagher continues: "In any case it is important that we recognize the newness of the situation within which faith has to be built. It needs new bricks and new methods of construction. In many respects the cultural tide has turned and will no longer offer support for religious faith. There is less reliance on authority and custom and much more on interiorization and commitment."

Karl Rahner describes recent church history as a time of "sacramental enthusiasm." His comments indicate that we have tended to think of grace as conceived too exclusively through sacraments. It is important for the faith-helper to discern the values people live by and to recognize their goodness. Gallagher often uses the Emmaus story to illustrate Jesus' acceptance of the disciple's version of the Crucifixion and Resurrection story. "They haven't understood but he wants to hear their version of His story. It is as if He has to allow them to express their own experience, even if they have the wrong end of the stick. . . . Only after they have expressed themselves and been heard are they ripe to hear the full horizon of God. Even toward the end of the story, after they had come to understanding, Jesus 'made as if to go another way' leaving them to go on to the village on their own. It is a question of freedom. They are given the chance of not continuing their relationship on the road; it is their invitation ('stay with us') that leads from heart listening to the sacrament of the table." They like many 21st century seekers who once were Catholics "lose hope that hope could ever again come alive in their lives."

Gallagher derives a model of faith-counseling from the Emmaus episode:

1. Walk genuinely with those who search, in solidarity and companionship along their road.

2. Listen with reverence to their stories and do not rush in with "the truth" before having heard them out.
3. Be ready to offer deeper vision, through scripture, of what they have experienced.
4. Respect their freedom to go further on the road of faith now or wait until the time is riper.
5. Let the sacraments be the crown of a careful human journey of search and honesty of dialogue.
6. Hope that they then can be fired with a mission to return to others and to share what they have discovered.

This process corresponds closely with the stages of the RCIA process. Gallagher recognizes that with many people today the first two stages are all that can be realistically expected in ministry with "unbelievers." He also recommends "the Fowler interview" found in the Appendix of *Stages of Faith* as useful for faith-helpers. It inquires into turning points of life and experiences that contributed to one's position now, images of God, sin, death, prayer, change. Issues like "out of what level of self was anger coming?" Crucial issues like "which church" is being rejected need to be discerned. Frequently, such folks tend to "think about the Church" along obediential and legalistic lines (primarily about Sunday practice and sexual morality). This stereotype is amazingly common. Good things happen when the un-churched find themselves welcomed as they are. Gallagher makes it all explicit: there are many ways of belonging to the Church. The parable of the Last Judgment judges people only by the generosity of their lives. "Such a recognition coming from a Church person should never be mere strategy: it is a human truth, spoken in friendship and yet rooted in the trust that God's Spirit can be alive and active in people who have not yet come to fullness of Christian memory or belonging. The Church has something to offer to these victims of our cultural crisis." For the past fifty years the Church in its documents has always looked with reverence on those who seem to reject or ignore God. There has been reverence for God's hidden ways in each heart and life and a reverence for the conscience and freedom of each person.

In the diagram below Gallagher describes three situations of faith. There are implications here for churches intent on serious evangelizing processes.

Three situations for faith

	A	B	C
KIND OF SOCIETY	Stable,rural; older culture of obedience protected world	New affluence, media exposure; mobility of values	Urban non-community: technological, complex, class divided
POSITION OF CHURCH	Dominant, central institutional authority	Religion as one influence among others; more autonomy for human values	A marginal institution; relativity of world-views
TYPE OF "UNBELIEF" FOUND	Non-practice by marginal individuals	Alienation of sub-groups from inherited religion (youth, workers, etc.)	Widespread indifference; eclipse of sense of God
LANGUAGE OF FAITH	Belong to deep convention rooted in sacraments	Struggle for personal conviction, rooted in relationship to Christ	Option for different way of life; rooted in search for community and for justice

PASTORAL RESPONSES	Bring individuals back to sacraments	Renew church structures for better evangelization (small communities)	Critique of society; awaken basic question of God

Rahner warns us against the false impression that faith was widespread in column A societies.

Modern society pushes the need to develop people to Fowler's stage four. "Many people will need another wavelength or religion if their faith is to survive the trials of a more complex culture. Fowler's fourth stage is a faith of personal decision and less one of conventional belonging. The faith of stage four requires serious commitment, is less dependent on support structures and enables people to swim against the tide. We cannot avoid neglecting this hunger for an awareness of God's presence in the secularized world in which people live."

Gallagher summarizes four areas in which faith is in crisis today. First is the transition from passive church membership to an experience of the parish as fostering involvement and growth. The second is to recognize that faith is called to change history through a struggle for justice. The third is about the kind of personal faith development that moves people from convention to conviction, especially by finding more depth through Scripture reading and prayer. The fourth area is intellectual growth so that one can be honestly related to a more complex culture.

James, one of Gallagher's literary students puts it this way: "Not only did faith get reduced to religious duties, it also became divorced from being a way of courageous living. . . .We never heard, with any persuasiveness, that to be a follower of Christ means trying to confront the established values of the world. The Bible often spoke of idolatry, the falling for false gods. I think we're surrounded by systematic idolatry and it would be far too innocent if we failed to see that. The driving seat of our society is occupied by a system of values that is quietly subversive of Christianity: success, competition, the business ethic, economics-as-salvation and a powerful propaganda machine of glamour and gloss. If that is true it is ridiculous to think that all religion needs is a little bit of renewal. It needs to go on the offensive—not in a tone of moan but of active prophecy."

Rahner had thought in the 50s that we had entered a period "irreversibly secularized." To put so much weight on faith-as-choice asks that we make a giant leap from the inherited assumptions of most Church people. The question is how to enter contact at all with people whom we might presume are "religiously indifferent." Rahner again advises us to remember: the "already present and implicit grace within each individual." It is a matter of uncovering what is in people's hearts. "The grace of God has always been there ahead of our preaching. Hence, our preaching is not really an indoctrination with something alien from the outside but the awakening of something within, as yet not understood but nevertheless really present." Rahner's mystagogy focuses attention on those experiences in which the individual has the experience of being taken out of oneself (the transcendent experience). Gallagher cites Leopold de Reyes "unhelpful ways" believers approach the non-practicing. He finds them excessively rigid and authoritarian, excessively manipulating or coldly intellectually, aggressive or naively sentimental. Leopold deReyes is clear, only a relationship of mutual freedom and respect as equals can lead to fruitful interaction. Without deep respect and good listening any effort at evangelization is ill advised. Ultimately, it is about love. This is the "slow service" of the entire renewal of church spirituality.

3

Evangelization

❦

IN the last chapter I attempted to create a theological frame of reference for pastoral work today, especially for efforts to speak to those no longer actively involved in the life of the Church.

Meeting anyone at the level of an evangelical encounter means meeting them in the depth of their experience. Some, as in the Gospel, need to hear a particular message of Jesus. Everyone needs to be recognized and related to in the hope, love, and joy of the Gospel. Such respect and sensitivity for individual persons is the base from which evangelization needs to take place.

Because evangelization is such an ambiguous term in church discussions, let me begin by offering the working definition I will use in this chapter. Evangelization means any processes or actions that:

- awaken or nurture faith
- build the Church
- transform the world to be more like the world the Gospel describes

From the above definition any parish can see that it is already involved in these three aspects of evangelization. However, if one considers the concern about evangelization that has been expressed by recent popes and conferences of bishops it is obvious that present efforts are inadequate. In a class I took in the 1960s Josef Goldbrunner, a groundbreaking leader in the catechetical movement, described the situation in

Europe as "low tide" for the Church. That certainly became truer in subsequent years. At the opening of the 1974 Vatican Synod on Evangelization the bishops in attendance were asked to keep three questions in mind: "In our day what has happened to that hidden energy of the good news, which is able to have such a powerful effect on human conscience? To what extent and in what way is that evangelical force capable of really transforming the people of this century? What methods should be followed in order that the power of the Gospel may have its effect?"

The first two of these questions would be fine reflection questions for any group to begin a discussion of parish evangelization. To further personalize these questions one might ask those assembled to get in touch with those "hidden energies" and "evangelical forces" that have had a "powerful" and "transforming" effect in their own lives.

Pope John Paul II in "Vocation and Mission" set the mark high when he wrote, "The church today ought to take a giant step forward in its evangelization effort and enter a *new stage of history* in its missionary dimension." And in a 1984 speech entitled "Building A New Latin America" he called for a new "evangelization," "new in methods," "in expression," and "in ardor." "Ardor" would seem to imply enthusiasm, spirit, élan, imagination, and excitement. "Methods" in today's world point to more listening, more participation, more sharing in small groups, and more effective use of media and wider consciousness of the role of the Church in the world today. "Expression" implies using the language of today's people, valuing the "secular" and "ordinary" and uncovering their already existing spirituality. We have been over some of this ground in the first chapter. It is important that we take the above statement of John Paul II as an indication that we ought to be making serious new efforts in evangelization and realize that the methods and expression need to speak to the people in new and creative ways.

In December 1990 the Holy Father presented a more developed understanding of the new evangelization in his encyclical "On the Permanent Validity of the Church's Missionary Mandate." It is clear in this document that "new evangelization" was addressed to countries in which people had already been Christian. In the contemporary situation, the pope was challenging us to be "more imaginative so that the risen Christ might give more spirit to the Church."

In Luke's gospel Jesus' enthusiasm is clear: "God has sent me to bring good news to the poor, to proclaim good news to captives, recovery of sight to the blind, and release to prisoners." Jesus' encounter with the Samaritan woman epitomizes his stance towards other cultures and towards women. After the wondrous encounter with Jesus she goes back to her townspeople and all she says is: "Come and see a man who has told me everything I ever did." As Patrick Brennan observes: "all the encounters of Jesus hold attitudes and actions we need to adopt for evangelization in our time. He has the joy of the messenger of the Good News from God, the mercy and tenderness of one who loves concrete individual persons, the willingness to listen and enter their stories."

In a memorable passage in "Work and Evangelization," in *The New Catholic Evangelization*, John Haughey, S.J. encourages us to do as Jesus did:

> In fact, one could ask whether Jesus had evangelization, as it is usually practiced today as part of His agenda. As I have already observed, it is not even clear that He sought to bring His hearers into a faith other than the ones they already embraced. He was certainly not trying to make Jewish hearers disengage from their Jewish faith

and become Christians. What He did seek was to purify their understanding and hearts about the God they had believed in and whose mercy and goodness and love they had undoubtedly heard about but whom they hadn't come to wholly trust. Jesus exhorted them to a degree of trust and love of God that they had not previously imagined.

He seemed much more of an experiential aposteriorist about His ministry than a theoretical apriorist. By this I mean that Jesus seemed to take His cues about what His work was to be on a given day from what He discovered God already doing in those people and circumstances in which He found Himself. For example, He healed the man who was lying sick on his mat for thirty-eight years on the Sabbath because He found the compassion of God speaking to Him that day through the man and He acted upon it, 'since my Father is at work until now, and I am at work as well' (Jn 5:17). There is no indication that He had gone to the pool of Bethsaida with that particular work of healing in mind. It was prompted by what he discerned.

Jesus' way of going about evangelization is important to understand and imitate. Apriori evangelization knows too much about what the other or others ought to believe and too little about what they actually do believe. Aposteriori evangelization is a more reverent way of proceeding. It begins by listening, not speech. And it doesn't speak words about God or theological ideas. It speaks words that have already been eaten by the speaker, words that God has enabled the speaker to taste and digest, words coming from experiencing God actually at work in a given situation and person (Ez 3:1-4).

Jesus' experience with the Samaritan woman is a case in point. In this seemingly chance encounter by Jacob's well He discovers and uncovers 'everything I ever did' (Jn 4:29). Jesus is not described by John as having preached to her, only as having probed her, unearthing the things in herself she did not wish to look at, graces she had declined, the sins she had committed. She became a messenger to her townspeople, convincing them that here was someone so special they had to come and see for themselves. Subsequently, many came out to see Him and succeeded in having Him stay with them for the next two days. From what He taught them they came to believe 'that He really is the savior of the world' (Jn 4:42).

Still another aspect of Jesus' aposteriori way of evangelizing the people—His opening them up to God's in-breaking-reign—looks at what was going on in the evangelizer himself during the dialogue with the Samaritan woman. We know that He stopped at the well to get food because He was thirsty and that the apostles went off to get food because He and they were hungry. When they returned with the desired victuals He indicated that He had become indifferent to their food because 'I had food to eat of which you do not know' (Jn 4-32). His food was the joy of finding God at work in her soul. While He was evangelizing her, stripping away all defenses she had put up between herself and God, he found joy in the Lord, whose working in her He was able to uncover.

In both of these stories God was being uncovered and the depth dimension of faith as good news was experienced.

Michael Gallagher puts it well in a story he heard from the most saintly person he has ever known: the question asked was: "what difference does Christian faith make?" The man answered with a parable: "Suppose I asked you to carry a bag for me and leave it in a house down the road, and suppose you generously did that, that would be good. If you thought that there was just rubbish in the bag but you carried it because I asked you,that would be good. But if you knew there was gold in the bag, it would make a difference. To know the worth of what you are carrying changes everything." We are sent into life with the gold of God's light. I find it amazing that Jesus turned over the mission of God in this world to us, even if we realize, as Paul VI says: "that the Holy Spirit is the principal agent of evangelization in both each individual who proclaims the gospel and in those who accept it in the depth of conscience." I say this because unless evangelizing activities arise out of a profound respect for the world and a profound respect for persons it will always remain superficial.

At a Christmas party I attended once, the host invited me over to his table at dessert time. A friend of his wanted to talk to me about speaking to his wife who had recently been sporadic about Sunday Mass attendance. He thought she was giving bad example to their children. I could share that concern but didn't particularly want to become involved in this triangle under these circumstances. The husband pointed at her seated at table about thirty feet away. The pointing at was demonstratively insensitive. It seemed like an act of abuse: to invite me to "straighten her out" and then point at her as if she were an object was not the gracious act of a loving husband. She got up and as she came towards me all sorts of things ran through my mind. She looked like a gentle and kind woman. I'm stuck— I'm supposed to be some kind of moral arbiter and authority. What do I say? She looks like a person with whom one could have a conversation. Something is going on in her spiritual life.

I said: "It's a pleasure to meet you, Megan. Brian told me you have three girls who you really enjoy right now." Brian then introduced the dreaded subject: "Yeah, but she isn't going to church regularly anymore." She made a comment about some things in her life that were upsetting her Sunday schedule. I took that to be just a good defense for *right now*. Good for her! I went on by saying something like: "well I am glad life is good. God loves the unfolding of our stories." She looked at me with appreciation. I could see that she thought something like "he understands." I sensed that she was a very good woman. There was a quiet heroism about her. She may be having some church questions but they were not matters for accusation. I just welcomed the accused.

Parishioners involved in evangelization need to understand this deeply mysterious aspect of what they do. As St. Paul describes it: "speaking the wisdom of God in a mystery" (1 Cor 2:7). We are "to make known the mystery of the Gospel" (Eph 6:19). We are "dispensers of the mysteries of God" (1 Cor 4:1). He prays, "to be *shown opportunities* for announcing the message and proclaiming the mystery of Christ" (Col 4:3). It is God's mystery in the mysterious life of the other that we share when we encounter them in faith.

An Evolving Church in America

Our history in America as a Church has emphasized the preserving and the nurturing of the faith of immigrant Catholic people. Building the church is something we certainly did well for early Catholic immigrants. Research seems to indicate that Catholic education has gone a long way to foster more social justice concern among Catholic people than in the general population. As previous generations of Catholics received opportunities for higher education they have contributed greatly to mainstream American life. Anti-Catholic movements dampened proselytizing efforts during much of our history. There were the visionary efforts of Isaac Hecker and Walter Elliott and the Paulist efforts in 19th century America to speak to wider audiences, but we have generally been wary and very timid about reaching out to those not of our congregations. For most of my lifetime "evangelization" has been a Protestant word and still connotes ringing doorbells or approaching people on the street as Mormons and Jehovah Witnesses do. As one evangelical writer says, "most people don't want to be gifted in evangelization and they don't want to sit next to one." For most Catholics, evangelization is tantamount to invading another's privacy. Whenever I heard the word evangelization as a child it meant "making Catholics" in the "missions," i.e., far away.

However, the children and grandchildren of immigrant populations presented different challenges for the institutional Church. The 60s brought a confusing set of complexities. The rediscovery of "the natural" (in contrast to a more otherworldly spirituality), the desire for more personal religious experience, the desire for more participation, the search for greater depth of understanding, and the voluntary nature of American religion all seem to converge simultaneously. It was a time when impersonal, institutional, dogmatic, authoritarian, and clerical categories were being rejected by young Catholics. Eugene Kennedy puts it well when he describes younger Catholics saying "yes" to hierarchy, ritual, and dogma but needing their Church "to be more personal, experiential, affective, and thoughtfully involved." That is a synthesis that is still in progress among Catholic laity.

In order to be more effective in larger parishes (above 700 members) we need to learn how to do "big church better." Lyle

Schaller, mainline Protestant Church writer and consultant to churches has found that the "rule of 200" applies in all size churches. No matter what size the local church may be, leadership people tend to know only 200 people well. All churches seem to do quite well in reaching that core group of believers. The task remains to create environments and opportunities for building "lateral relationships and ministries" among parishioners—doing "big Church" better.

From protecting the faith of immigrants we had graduated to what a young priest in my mother's parish called "saving the saved" in the 40-year period since the 60s. However, we have lost multitudes of baptized Catholics from Catholic practice. We will take up this question a little later in the chapter. Leadership people love to see people return after choosing to be absent. Parishes love to see R.C.I.A. candidates become Catholic at the Easter Vigil but we have not sought out those who have left—in any serious way. We must acknowledge that our evangelical effort has been inadequate in two significant areas.

1. *Seeking out the lost:* A few years ago I was very pleased by the wonderful mission statement of the Catholic Charities Office in the diocese of Rockville Centre. It read: "to find the people who hurt the most, and need the most to break down the prejudices and stereotypes that prevent you from engaging with them, to help them in the most dignified way possible, to seek and confront whatever causes their hurt in the first place, to fix the systems and situations that hold them back and leave them with more power in their lives, and to do it all with your feet in the parish, connected to a Eucharistic community guided by social Catholic teaching."

2. The second area where we fail is right at our doorstep: *taking the next step in parish ministries*. The best example is the neglect of outreach to parents who send their children to Catholic school or to religious education and are no longer active Church members. Why is this so? Why do most parishes not engage parents in discussion? In one such discussion I had with a parish staff, they gave the following possible reasons for parental lack of participation:

- They have had no religious education themselves.
- They had been raised as nominal Catholics and their own families never practiced.
- They have had marital and sexual freedom issues and saw the Church as repressive of sexuality.
- They were practicing contraception and felt guilty about going to Communion.
- They had not integrated into the community and did not feel needed.
- They were married, divorced, and remarried civilly.
- They may have had an abortion and thought they were excommunicated.
- They were alienated from the Church and experienced it as cold, distant and, authoritarian.
- They had a hurtful Church experience.
- They were lax, lazy and indifferent.

This is not an exhaustive list but a fairly representative one. After a brief discussion, the group grew in understanding and appreciation of the complexity of the parents' low participation in church life. They seemed to grow in sympathy for those with whom they had been angry only a few minutes earlier. They were more ready for understanding and helpful responses to these parents. Evangelization of parents became an option now. In any case, they would have to get beyond their complaining and negativity and become more sensitive and creative. This core group of catechists represented parishioners who were fairly conventional in their thinking about those who were different. The group moved on and saw that they needed to make more use of "sensing interviews" at the time of registration and sacramental occasions. As yet there wasn't any decision on direct efforts to reach these parents, but they would be more understanding and more appreciative of their own work and willing to engage in discussion of what they might do to reach out to these parents. The catechists needed additional understanding of their role with these families. These catechists could possibly realize the call to be helpers rather than frustrated complainers.

The Evangelical Approach

While I was writing this chapter a friend asked me why I thought the newly founded mega-churches (like Willow Creek, Saddlebrook, New Hope) have been so successful at attracting members. Of course, there are multiple reasons. One could say such churches are less demanding morally and dogmatically and more akin to the American spirit: democratic, free, more communitarian. But I think research shows that it is primarily because they build their congregations on the expressed needs of their people. Most Catholic parishes don't provide the same opportunities for people to express their needs and concerns in any systematic inclusive way. Even when we have done consulting at the national level on needs and concerns and produce documents and resources, we tend not to implement or involve people at the local level. The best example I know is the wonderful "Plan of Pastoral Action for Family Ministry" approved and published by the United States Council of Catholic Bishops in 1978. It was a hopeful, inspiring and very practical document. In it the bishops outlined six areas of pastoral ministry to married couples: ministry for pre-married and single people, ministry for married couples, ministry to parents, ministry for "developing" families, ministry for "hurting" families, ministry to leadership couples and families. Appendix A at the end of this chapter gives some typical examples of activities from the bishop's document. I remember reading this plan and admiring its authors. The whole question of family life was the right question for parishes at that time. The six categories seemed so obviously correct. Parishes could build a program in each of the areas (it might be necessary to prioritize among the six). Nothing significant ever came of this at the parish level. In 1990 the bishops published "Family Ministry, a Pastoral Plan and Reaffirmation." It was just that, a "reaffirmation" and reminder of the 1978 document.

These most useful documents could have been implemented. They made sense. They were obviously based on long, hard, intelligent data-based work by knowledgeable people and approved unanimously by the bishops. It was at that point I lost hope that we could ever expect that this kind of document would ever be more than a resource for the highly proactive pastor. There was no accountability, discussion, participation or local decision making to make systematic family life processes an active component of parish life. In chapter four "On Young People Today" we will see a similar pattern in dealing with youth and young adult ministry.

A few years ago I was struck by the titles of a few books by George Hunter III: *How to Reach Secular People* and *Church For the Un-churched*. Hunter does research and writes particularly for the so-called "seeker churches," like the mega churches mentioned earlier. He finds that the barriers to church growth are more sociological and cultural than anything else. There are three myths about modern secular people held by church people that Hunter finds untrue: 1) that religious consciousness is being erased from people's minds and we are entering a period of "no religion"; 2) that people are more immoral today; 3) that sophisticated, educated modern people have rejected Christian teaching. He finds on the contrary, there are signs of great interest in religion, though there is a great menu of religious options that the Church no longer controls. Secular people also participate in many moral struggles and make many moral choices. They are, however, less programmed by Christian enculturation. They get the premises for their moral decisions most often from parents, peers and popular culture. And as for being educated and sophisticated, let us not believe it. Hunter believes that most people are more naïve and not religiously sophisticated at all. Many of their opinions come from popular culture and the media.

Hunter describes three groups who have now become the vast mission field of the Church in the western world:

- Ignostics (about 1/3) who have no Christian memory—that is, they don't know what Christians are thinking about even though they may have had some early religious education.
- Notional Christians (about 1/3) who think of themselves as more or less Christian because they assume their culture is more or less Christian and they fit in to some sort of public Christianity.
- Nominal Christians (about 1/3) who are somewhat active in their churches but most of the gospel "washes past them." Their life has no Christian agenda as such.

The most important thrust in all these "seeker" churches is simply a great compassion for lost and pre-Christian people.

Bill Hybels, pastor of Willow Brook frames his church's message with these two affirmations: 1) "You matter to God, no matter how far you have fallen, no matter how many of his laws you have broken." 2) "The Christian life is not just a way to prepare to die. It is a better way to live, the straightest, truest path toward human fulfillment, even though it is very demanding and challenging along the way." Rick Warren of Saddleback Church in Texas puts it this way: 1) "that God is a personal God, and cares about you and your life; He wants a relationship with you, in which He knows you and you know Him; 2) that God is in control and that the things that are out of your control are not out of His control; 3) that you cannot control the things that happen to you, but with the Holy Spirit's guidance and power, you can control your responses."

The clear approach of seeker churches is to put emphasis on the following eight pastoral areas: Scriptural preaching, Bible study, personal prayers, a vision of what people can become, small groups, gift-based lay ministry, conversation with someone gifted in shepherding ministry, and music, style and language adapted to the population. Churches with these emphases create a more apostolic laity. Hunter concludes that the weakness of much of mainline church life in America today comes from the fact that " 'it doesn't scratch where people itch', that it images a boring rule-bound life, and that parishioners love tradition more that the surrounding community." It makes all the difference in the world when a congregation feels like it is on a mission to the lost and needy.

One of the great learnings that Hunter describes is that people in such churches that seek out the lost is that they discover the reality of "prevenient" grace (a term from St. Augustine that describes grace already present in people before becoming

Christian). Hunter puts it this way: "that in every season God's spirit is preparing the hearts of some people to receive the Gospel. It is always 'harvest time'; the Spirit can always find receptive people."

There is much for us to learn in the writings of those involved in building successful large churches in America today. I found George Hunter a good place to start.

Lyle Schaller reminds us that in the year 2000, although the data base was incomplete, somewhere between 15 to 20 million adults, second through fifth generation American-born Catholics, had left the Church. About one-half are now members of Protestant congregations and the other half are "sitting on the sidelines and waiting." Much of the growth in churches is beyond the mainstream. Growth has not been in Catholic, Lutheran, Episcopal, Presbyterian, Methodist, and older Baptist churches. What are called "American Originals": Seventh-Day Adventists, The Evangelical Free Church of America, Assemblies of God, numerous Baptist associations, plus thousands of autonomous non-denominational churches, all show growth. The usual Catholic interpretation of this data attributes the "falling away" to the Church's strong stand on the sexual questions of birth control, divorce and remarriage, homosexuality, abortion, and our image as authoritarian and autocratic. I think, rather, that much has to do with lack of a more personal approach to members and the failure to engage the gifts of our members sufficiently.

Schaller cites Robert Randall's book *What People Expect From Church* and says that attractiveness of churches comes down to having a clear emphasis. The parish church needs to fulfill four needs:

1. the yearning to feel understood
2. the yearning to understand

3. the yearning to belong

4. the yearning for hope

All four of these expectations are essentially about communication and relationships, not tasks or functions. Schaller sees that a creative effort needs to be made in the skills of evangelism: i.e., listening skills, Bible study, and those skills involved in knowing how to "do big church." He expects, that with help, congregations will grow to as much as four times their size. Whether or not you share such high expectations, I think we have to consider carefully Jesus' challenge that "the harvest is ripe."

Some Models for Catholic Evangelization

I have found that the most useful activity to begin any work with those interested in evangelization is reflection on their own experience of receiving "the good news" in their life. When I have led groups discussing evangelization I always begin with shared prayer around Luke's Christmas narrative. I ask the group to reflect for some time on two questions: Who was it that brought the "good news" to you in your life? What did they do? This reflection will always elicit the memory of some few people who appeared in each person's life who were highly significant because of their sensitivity, understanding and kindness. Telling the "good news" stories of parents, relatives, teachers and friends recalled joys once experienced and brought to mind again this deep personal appreciation. An uncle, a wondrous third grade teacher, a lame elderly neighbor with an ever-present smile, and a great father showed them the way. Evangelization had happened through these messengers. They knew that God had visited them. This gave them hope, joy and enthusiasm for life.

Small group faith sharing is one of the most useful frameworks for rebuilding faith and participation. Patrick Brennan in his book *Re-Imagining the Parish*, describes the pioneering work of Drs. Cho and Hurston in South Korea in forming OIKOS groups, (OIKOS being the Greek word in the New Testament for "household"). As this approach has been developed by the staff of St. Boniface parish in Pembroke Pines, Florida, "household" includes four kinds of groups.

1. Kinship groups—those who are related to us by family ties
2. Geographical location groups—those who live in our immediate neighborhood
3. Interest groups—those who share our concerns and hobbies
4. Vocational groups—those to whom we relate at work

Most people have about 200 people in their OIKOS circle. Putting together John Haughey's description of Jesus' approach to people and understanding the make-up of OIKOS groups in one's own life makes "evangelizing " efforts a most personal process.

In the previous chapter we reviewed Michael Gallagher's stages of "faith counseling." We need to pay attention (as many fundamentalist and evangelical churches do) to training competent "faith helpers." Susan Blum has made both group work such as OIKOS and the kind of companioning described by Gallagher required preparation training for evangelization. In her essay, "The Need for Evangelization Training," Blum asks whether old Catholics (or the old institutional Church) learns new tricks. What she calls "relational counselors" (i.e., laity involved in informal evangelistic encounters) have many opportunities for listening to others. This is the most basic form of evangelization. Susan describes six programs for training those called to parish evangelization. One of them, the National Council for Catholic Evangelization, divides training into "Creating A Vision for Catholic Evangelization" and "Skills for Evangelization Teams." The new awareness needs to be supported with skills, particularly ongoing training in listening skills. Pope Paul VI in his encyclical on *Evangelization in the Modern World* called for "a serious preparation" in all workers for evangelization. Patrick Brennan reminds us that "most parish leadership needs significant retooling to do the work of evangelization." And: "training which largely is done by a re-imagined staff, is a profoundly spiritual activity. Ministerial training ought to take 50 to 75 percent of a staff's time, if the staff is truly enabling." I designed such a listening training program when I was facilitating a gift discernment process at the parish level. I know of two parishes that have trained a group of parish listeners. Much is possible here. Carol Gura in "Models for An Evangelizing Parish" suggests that the evangelization team will need to search, read, and study the work of other parishes and denominations for "best practices." The team would benefit most if it "gathers the leaders of ministries for dialogue and creative development." The most essential of these evangelizing ministries include: RCIA, small group leaders, social justice groups, re-membering Church groups, bereavement groups, divorced and separated groups, spiritual development committees, adult enrichment groups, and family ministry leaders.

Patrick Brennan puts it this way: "the Catholic Church in most places does not have adequate structure for evangelizing." The National Plan for Hispanic Ministries calls evangelization our greatest challenge and recognizes the need "to take serious steps to plan, set goals and equip people with skills."

These three challenges are very clear. In the pages that follow I will offer some approaches that might be most fruitful. I have always found the template of Joseph Fichter, S.J. very helpful.

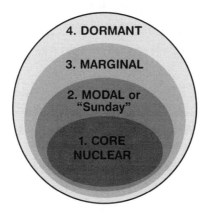

In the model above, Fichter divides Church membership into four groupings (I have added a fifth: The Un-baptized) and describes them in the following manner:

1. Nuclear Catholics
   - Are completely faithful to religious practice
   - Are very active in the social life of the parish
   - Tend not to be integrated into the life of the secular culture

2. Modal Catholics
   - Keep Sunday observance in Church
   - Live with a "middling" sort of religious practice
   - Do not take much part in parish activities

3. Marginal Catholics
   - Are irregular in practice (10-12 times a year)
   - May participate in some parish functions
   - Are not integrated in any sub group

4. Dormant Catholics
   - Are almost totally inactive
   - Have not joined another Church (This was Fichter's description in the 1960-70s. Today it seems that many dormant Catholics have joined other churches.)
   - Are strongly integrated into the life of the secular world
5. The Un-baptized
   - Those who have never been baptized. In the vignette cited previously in which catechists discerned why parents might be fairly inactive in their faith it was clear that they needed to be sympathetic and to reach out to them. Evangelization is first of all an attitude and then a relationship. Gallup in studying "the un-churched American" gave four lines of needed development: 1) that churches start processes to reach out to the inactive and un-churched; 2) that greater experimentation be given to family evangelization; 3) that small groups within the parish be supported and facilitated; 4) that institutional models of the Church be stressed less so that religious experience can be encouraged more.

Another model akin to Fichter's was developed by Philip Murnion of the National Pastoral Life Center, who found that Paul VI's encyclical "On Evangelization" named four kinds of evangelization activity:

1. Deepening the faith of the active (Fichter's Nuclear model)
2. Outreach to the inactive (Fichter's Marginal and Dormant)
3. Outreach to the un-churched (the un-Baptized and non-practicing)

4. Bringing Gospel values to society (all the social implications of the Gospel of our time)

To recognize all efforts to "bring Gospel values to society," Paul VI's perspective inserts the parish into the evangelization of the culture. "It is a question of not only preaching the Gospel" in ever wider geographical areas but also of affecting and as it were upsetting: "mankind's criteria of judgment, point of interest, lines of thought, and sources of inspiration and models of life." Each of these aspects needs to be discerned by those who lead evangelization efforts. In the next chapter I will illustrate some of these challenges that need to be made to our culture from the work of David Walsh.

Mark Chopro of the General Council of the U.S.C.C. listed twenty areas that are of high concern to American Bishops.

Abortion	Food and agriculture
Arms control/arms trading	Health, AIDS, substance abuse
Capital punishment	Housing
Communications	Human rights
Racism and discrimination	Immigration
The economy	International affairs
Education	Refugees
Environmental justice	Regional concerns
Euthanasia	Welfare
Families and children	Violence

There are parishioners who are passionately concerned about some of these matters. They are meant to be leaders by making parishioners aware of the church's concern for the urgent needs of our world and by stimulating parish action. We need these Spirit-inspired people to come forth among us. I know a parish that includes a weekly column in the parish bulletin written by a retired social studies teacher. Over the years he has written columns on most of these concerns. Parish initiatives have resulted. The prophetic agenda needs to be kept before the parish on a regular basis. Group discussion around issues of justice and peace could provide impetus in the parish for continued involvement with the Church's teaching on social justice.

Finally, I am including two lists of the most successful evangelization efforts in the United States today. The first is from Patrick Brennan; the second is based on my own experience.

Most Successful Evangelization Efforts: Patrick Brennan

1. Small-based communities
2. RCIA and Remembering the Church
3. Adult Faith Formation programs
4. Family-Centered Religious Education
5. Efforts at social justice

My Own List of Additional Successful Evangelization Efforts

1. Participation and follow up on sacramental moments (e.g., Elizabeth ministry for new parents)
2. Scripture study groups
3. The Charismatic movement
4. Gift discernment programs
5. The Cursillo movement
6. Door-to-door evangelization
7. Appointing block captains with pastoral responsibility to foster more personal contact
8. Parish visitor programs
9. Re-entry processes (e.g., Landings where returning Catholics review their beliefs)
10. Bereavement ministry, ministry of consolation
11. Lifeteen efforts, and Theology on Tap for young adults

It is important for parishes today to determine their evangelization priorities and to plan strategies to reach out to the many who thirst for lifegiving waters. We need to "find the people who hurt the most and need the most."

ᘍᘍ

Appendix A

Ministry for Premarrieds and for Single People

A. Single People

Support groups for young singles

Support groups, societies and associations for single people

Retreat programs

(Note the importance of the vocation of lifelong singles, and the single-again, who also should not be forgotten in "family" ministry and who need primary community.)

B. Engaged Couples

Pre-Cana

Engaged Encounter or Tobit weekends

Remote and proximate preparation for marriage

Couple-sponsor ministry

Ministry for Married couples

Newlywed ministry

Anniversary programs and liturgies

Marriage enrichment in parish-centered programs

Marriage Encounter

Natural family planning

Family financial planning

Spiritual direction programs for couples

Life in retirement years of marriage

Marriage retreats

Ministry for parents
   Parenthood education programs
   Beginning parent (family) program
   Parent counseling services
   Teen-parent communications
   Expectant parents' program
   Adopt a grandparent
   Single parenting
   Right to life counseling
   Parent catechist formation
   Parental classes (for sacrament preparation and home
      worship)
   Parent-School Association/Guild

Ministry for "Developing" Families
   Family Life-Cycle Education
   Parent-infant education
   Family weekends
   Parish family enrichment programs
   Family spiritual development groups
   Family cluster and growth groups
   Family neighborhood networks
   Parish family liturgies
   Family social action programs
   Family living and sexuality education
   Aging family programs

Ministry for "Hurting" Families
   Parish family counseling
   Bereaved family programs
   Family reconciliation projects

Right to Life groups
Substance (drugs and alcohol) abuse programs for families
Beginning Experience
Handicapped Encounter Christ (HEC) programs for families
Aging in-home care programs
Social service and social action for families/by families

Ministry for Leadership Couples and Families
Leadership training and development programs
Parish leadership communication formation
Skills training for family leaders
Specialized skills programs for leadership in various family ministries
Parent-Teacher Associations
Burn-out prevention programs for the actively involved
Clergy-lay teamwork support groups
Parish coordinator couple programs

4

The Challenge of Youth Today

⊙ᠭ᠊᠊᠊ᠬᠥ

I GREW up in a very large Catholic parish in Brooklyn, one of the five boroughs of New York City. It was a parish administered by a religious order, the Redemptorists. It was also a center for their work in the area. There were about thirty priests and a few brothers in residence. Just about all of them were active in some way in parish life. The parish elementary school, which I attended, enrolled about three thousand boys and girls and had a waiting list. Tuition was practically nothing, due to the fact that it was staffed by the Sisters of St. Joseph as teachers. Later, a girl's high school would be added, and in its heyday my parish would have about sixty sisters in residence.

My neighborhood was truly a neighborhood. On my street there were about 150 families living in attached three-story houses. As a child I knew all these people by sight and we took for granted a certain interest in each other's welfare. Nobody on my street ever got divorced (I remember my mother whispering to my grandmother one day about someone three streets away getting a divorce. It was somewhat scandalous to them). There were no drugs yet; no storekeepers would sell beer to kids; sex was pretty much under wraps although flirting was high. World War II was raging and I remember as a pre-teen being very interested in the daily radio and newspaper accounts of our progress. I knew that history was happening in a big way and, early in the war, survival was both a concern and a fear in my life.

My father was a most beloved person to me, a model of quiet, gentle ways to all people. He had been an immigrant and owned a medium-sized grocery store in the days before supermarkets became widespread. The worldwide depression was underway before his marriage to my mother and times were hard for him in the early days. He worked over seventy hours a week in the store all through my childhood. His customers had been badly hit by the depression and "paying when and if you could" became the way of doing business. He went about his work admirably. Every three-year-old was royalty when they came with a penny for candy. He was open and kind to everyone. My mother was a rather demanding woman. I was an only child and got a lot of attention from her. My maternal grandmother lived with us and was most understanding of me growing up. I had to perform well in school; it went without question. In the long run it probably was good for me.

It was an easy world in which to be a child. I don't think being an adolescent is ever going to be easy because of the amount of "finding" yourself that is thrust upon you. Add to the usual erotic and self issues of adolescence, the life choices of school and occupation had to be made earlier at that time. College was not a taken-for-granted-next-step after high school. You had to consider yourself a full adult at eighteen, and lots of the girls I knew were married at nineteen or twenty.

My church, because of the size of its religious staff and well-developed participation by the people of the parish, had all sorts of services. We had a youth program and even a building devoted to us called the parish club. There were basketball teams for all ages, a teenage dance every Friday night, bowling alleys (fifteen cents a game), pool, ping-pong tables and teenagers just hanging out. It was open every night and you could drop in at anytime.

This world no longer exists in the United States and at present I see no sign that it will or could return without some major disasters that would bring us back to simpler living. There could be nostalgia for this easier world but nostalgia will not help us now. The first thesis of this chapter is that American culture underwent revolutionary change in the 1960s and the church in the United States has been unable to engage young people since then. Later in this chapter I will describe my own experience as a high school religion teacher during that time. It is important for us to realize now that when Pope John Paul II spoke of "the new evangelization": "new in methods," "new in expression," and "new in ardor," he was asking us to seriously reconsider how we need to go about our work of evangelizing the young people of our time. It would be good to take some time just to reflect on those three expressions. It does imply that much of the "old" is not working. He also spoke of the effort to discover the language in which to reach people in their depth as "a cultural and evangelical project of first importance." We ought to take these words literally and seriously.

Selfhood: A Vital Entry Point for Christian Faith

As I started to write this chapter two old songs came to mind, Sammy Davis' "I Gotta Be Me" and Frank Sinatra's "My Way." I am in sympathy with those two sentiments and have always enjoyed people who wanted to be faithful to their uniqueness. In earlier times social conditioning prevented most people from experiencing and expressing much of themselves. Long hours of routine work, economic systems that didn't offer ways out of expected roles, lack of educational opportunity all have played a significant part in limiting people. In contrast, today's young people have many opportunities and possibili-

ties. Where a young person will live, what they will do, what
ethnic group they may marry into is wide open. "What they
will be" is a deeper and more important question. If inner
growth, personal happiness, and a worthwhile life are mea-
sures, then very little may depend on external opportunities.
We now know that those things are about the presence of goodness and love. All of the people of the world, from whatever era
and class have, more or less, equal opportunity. Abraham and
Sara, Isaac and Rebecca, Jacob and Rachel, Peter and Paul,
Mary and Mary Magdalene were not limited in their personhood by career openings, travel possibilities or technology.

However, "individuality" has been a growing concern since
the Renaissance. Charles Taylor, the Canadian Catholic
philosopher, has traced the making of the modern identity in
Sources of the Self. The earliest philosophers had concentrated
on "what it is right to do" rather then what "it is good to be."
St. Augustine in the fourth century is the first to wrestle open-
ly with his personal identity questions. As a man who struggled mightily with himself before becoming a Christian, he
now struggled with Christian identity—questions like what
our participation and likeness to the Trinity mean for personal
identity. But for Augustine the road to understanding both God
and ourselves must pass through attending to our inner selves.
"Do not go outward; return within yourself. In the inward man
dwells truth." What we need lies within ("intus"), he says
again and again. Augustine is fascinated by the inner light,
which can shine within when we are present to ourselves. God,
for Augustine is at our very core and can meet the person in
his/her depth.

It would be Michel de Montaigne, the seventeenth century
Renaissance essayist, who would renew Augustine's refrain.
Self-exploration will again become central to culture. The

assumption behind modern self-exploration will be that we don't already know who we are. Montaigne will always remain an orthodox Catholic but as a true son of the Renaissance he will not sell himself short on the right to explore his particular human life and what it tells him. "The limits which are relevant for me are mine." The struggle for us, Montaigne maintains, is for us to accept who we are. He recognizes that we must "live within human limits" but we need to explore, appreciate and learn ourselves. He warns against a spirituality that is excessive and tyrannical and depreciates and crushes the body. Taylor comments, "what it ends up with is an understanding of my own demands, aspirations, desires, in their originality, however much these may lie athwart the expectations of society and my immediate inclinations." The exploration of the self in order to come to terms with oneself has become one of the fundamental themes of modern culture. "How am I to enjoy my being loyally" is how Montaigne puts the question. For many who were raised to take the presence of the Church in their lives for granted, this highly personal approach might seem risky. It is now the only way that many who have been baptized Catholics in the last fifty years should be approached. David Schindler, a theologian and editor of the journal "Communio," a rather conservative Catholic scholarly publication, sums the situation up quite well when he calls us to recognize that the "subjective wing of modernity, with its innovative sense of selfhood, remains not only redeemable but a vital entry point for Christian faith in today's culture."

Thomas Merton had raised the distinction between the true and false self when discussing the modern identity problem. He raised the question this way: "if you want to identify me, ask me not where I live, or what I like to eat or how I comb my hair but ask me what I think I am living for in detail, and ask

me what I think is keeping me from living for the thing I want
to live for. Between these two answers you can identify any
person. The better answer he has, the more of a person he is."
Following Montaigne and Merton one should reflect deeply on
our desires, hopes and aspirations, qualities and talents and
attempt to live from their source. These questions have usually
been asked first in early adolescence. Today, there are many
competing voices in the world and within the young that prevent facing deeper personal questions. It is important to
approach the young personally on their discoveries and to provoke such questions when they seem to be non-existent. We
will have much more to say about this as we go along.

As Church we might try to live in a previous age where we
had a body of truth we wished to communicate and a body of
docile believers waiting to be informed. We need to believe that
if we can create the right settings and approach the young personally the promised light of the Holy Spirit is still quite capable of entering their consciousness. For the first three centuries
of the Church people became Christians because of personal
conviction. The mass baptisms of tribes from the fifth to ninth
centuries skewed our expectation about the need for personal
choice. The immigrant Catholic Church in the United States
found a lot of group identity in being Catholic together. Their
children began to loosen those bonds in an American culture
that was undergoing so much change in the 60s. Until the
middle half of the twentieth century there was no such thing as
a "teenager." In previous centuries children were seen as "little
adults" (see Neil Postman, *The Disappearance of Childhood*).
"Teenagers" began to appear in the 1950s when affluence was
on the rise in middle-class America. Affluence increased at the
same time as the rise of image media. Writers have shown that
films and music made especially for a teenage audience began

to appear around 1958. By 1964 we were talking about "the generation gap." A writer in the *New York Times Magazine* identified the crucial ingredients that made for the new phenomenon: "ultimately the product of an affluent society which, for the first time in history has made possible a leisure class of professional teenagers."

The Selling of Identity

As we said above, adolescence and the years of early adulthood have always been a time of "finding oneself" (identity issues) and finding a significant life-partner (intimacy issues). However, from the 1960s there were decided media efforts, driven by advertising money, to separate young people from the ethos of adult society. Quentin Schultze, professor of communication arts at Calvin College, puts it this way: "producers eagerly embraced the youth market, incessantly and profitably reworking its language, fads, fashions, mores, values, ideals, and dreams."

In recent years we have extended the process of "teenagerization" by creating a class of what we call "tweens" (originally would-be-teenagers between nine and twelve; recent research shows advertisers targeting the six to eight-year-old market). At the other end of the spectrum we have extended the "settling down" of youth into the mid-thirties. Author Robert Bly describes a common youth culture now embracing the twelve to thirty-five-year-old-age group where "adults regress toward adolescence and adolescents have no desire to become adults." Writing in 1996 Bly describes this age as not being able to imagine any genuine life coming from the past. In former societies tradition and religion had offered models for life. Now contemporary media and peers were to be the major sources for imitation. The young were not entering adulthood in the ways we had in previous centuries. We were an "other directed" society and the others were on our screens and in our music; popularity and conformity to peers became of prime importance. I am describing what Daniel Yankelovich, the renowned social scientist who, for the last half century has tracked changes in American culture, calls "the strong-formers" in this new culture; he leaves room for what he calls "weak formers," who were less influenced and held values from the older culture. It is a crucial distinction for what we will talk about as we go along in this chapter. Some recent research on "generations" indicates a significant falling away from media and peer culture in a larger percentage of those born after 1982. It will be interesting to watch that development. Christopher Lasch, another of the great students of American culture, had seen that indifference and devaluation of the past, "learning to need," and the failure to establish deep personal bonds were characteristics of the rise in narcissism that so marked this period. Lasch explains that the promotion of narcissism through selling images and impressions of being modern, current and chic is the most successful way to sell products. I find his judgments to be quite harsh but not without truth for the "strong formers" in the culture. For Bly it is a time in youth culture "where it is hard for parents to know how to approach one's children, what values to teach them and what to stand up for. There is a tendency among adults to go along with the young "where they are."

Bly will come down on the side of what he calls "the third brain," that traditionally is associated with "enlightenment." We have lower brain regions to take care of survival and emotional needs ("reptilian" and "limbic"). When we see the golden halo around the head of Christ and the saints we are being shown the sign of the third brain—wise and understanding and appreciative about life. It is the state, which all thoughtful parents hope for in their children's development. It is a difficult road in 21st century Western culture. I am reminded of the blessing of fathers at the end of the baptismal rite: "you are the first teachers; may you be the best of teachers." Somewhere within them, Christian parents hope this light will be upon them and their children. It is our responsibility as a Church to assist them.

A large part of this chapter is devoted to the discussion of the influence of American culture today on American Christians. I use the word "culture" to mean the image of *how life is to be lived, the practices and assumptions that exist in society.* Practices like greeting one's neighbor, wearing neckties in business settings, wearing veils or headscarves by Muslim women, are exterior manifestations of a belief system. There is also a concealed set of subjective attitudes that carry assumptions, values and meanings such as "whites are superior," "men are smarter," "money is the highest value." Individuals are largely unaware of what assumptions are hidden; small children especially are totally unaware of the practices and hidden assumptions of their society. For children it is just the way things are. The culture into which we are born is the "normal" program. "This is the way things are done around here." There is an "of courseness" about money and popularity being the most important values of adolescents and young adults. This was confirmed during a children's homily (7-12year olds) at Sunday Mass after asking them what they thought was the most important thing about life in the United States. A chorus responded immediately "money." A few mentioned family. We have certainly been led to believe in the last two generations that we need a lot of things. Of course, we need air condition-

ing at home and in our automobiles. Of course, children need
their own television and computer. We now have an immense
need list in middle-class America that I never imagined when
young. They may be good things, "wants," but certainly not
needs. And so, we have developed a consumer society in the
last sixty years. Both Christian and secular critics use the term
"consumerism and consumer capitalism" with disdain. I never
heard any discussion of consumer society when I was young.
Productivity was the by-word of the culture in which I grew
up.

Pope John Paul II in *Centesimus Annus* (1991) describes his
concern about "consumerism":

A given culture reveals its understanding of life
through the choice it makes in production and consumption. Here the phenomenon of consumerism arises. Of
itself, an economic system does not possess criteria for
correctly distinguishing new and higher forms of satisfying needs from artificial new needs *that hinder the formation of a mature personality. Thus a great deal of educational
and cultural work is urgently needed,* including the education of consumers in the responsible use of their power
choice . . . it is not wrong to want to live better; what is
wrong is a style of life presumed to be directed towards
"having" rather then "being."

These are powerful words for us to reflect on as we imagine
developing ways to approach discussion of consumption on
the parish level. An even more shocking statement can be
found in Pope John Paul's 1999 World Day of Peace address.
He said then that consumerism is "no less pernicious" than
"racism, Marxism, Nazism and Fascism." That statement
might seem a bit over the top to most of us. But Pope John Paul
II knew well the price that poor countries must pay to supply

the desires of the affluent society. As one social critic says, children in a poor country often become "little soldiers, little prostitutes and little factory workers" to survive.

I find Vincent Miller, professor of theology at Georgetown University, most enlightening in understanding the dynamics of consumerism. In *Consuming Religion* Miller explains that many writers explain consumerism as arising from a set of beliefs or values—"comfort is good," "more is better, "status rises with more things." Miller sees it differently. He puts it this way: "while excessive consumption is widespread, crass selfishness is not. Relatively few of us avow anything of this sort." For example, Miller says, "people would never explicitly choose such high levels of consumption if they were to face the privation of others." Not to know the evil consequences of our over-consumption is often interpreted as denial or self-deception—that may be the case. His unique contribution to the discussion is there might be a third reason: "we simply don't know what to do" and give up. People who drive SUVs that get twelve miles to a gallon may not like that but they still make the choice. We know that many farm workers are treated shamefully but we can't be expected to know about unfortunate circumstances behind each item in our grocery basket. We know that much of what is now made in China is made by prisoners in labor camps and children who often work 14 hours a day, seven days a week to keep factories running. What can we do?

It is obvious we need both government and watchdog organizations to help us. However, the larger question has to do with three issues which we need to bring into the consciousness of our people: concern for others in the world who are affected by our excessive consumption, the shallow life developed by subordinating ourselves to things, and the failure to overcome superficial desires and participate in the transformation of self. These are simply aspects of living the life of a sensitive disciple in this century.

What we need to be most concerned about with all young people is that they live what is inside of them, that they fulfill *their* possibility. It is not that I imagine that anyone has a clear idea of what potential for development exists within them. Self-knowledge of any direct sort eludes us. But as we unfold and develop in childhood there are many hints of our natural gifts. What I think we would all hate is the corruption of our children by others for personal gain. We trust the general goodness of our children's nature. We try to provide experiences in which they can grow. We put limits on them for their own good and we deeply want to protect them from negative experiences. Advertisers want to be a player in the area of our children's lives and are very clever players. They do a lot of research about selling to children, i.e., manipulating their desires. As one writer puts it: "every child has three parents." As Bly says, "we don't realize when we put a computer or a television in a child's room we are sending a child to be alone with the Giant." We never invite strangers to be alone with our children yet we allow so many strangers to be with our children when they are alone with manipulative advertisers.

The battle zone for the faith of the young is in the imagination. How children, adolescents and young adults imagine what Jesus and the Church stand for does not seem to contradict the values of consumer society. Most parents I meet are very naïve about the effect of the media and the constant materialistic consumer message to their children.

In *The Code of Advertising* Sut Jhally makes the case that both Marx and Freud saw that the rise of a consumer society was creating idolatrous forms of life. He sees that "people search for meaning in the domain of the commodity world. Within this context of a world without meaning wherein people search for meaning, arises the religion of use-value, the religion of advertising . . . its ability to mediate the dialectic of emptying and needing." Prompted by things Jhally said, I watched television commercials for a week from the point of view of "buying" happiness and perfection. Advertisers as a group would really like to fill up your unfilled longings. I think we are quite close to the very business of religion itself here.

If we had any doubt of our need as Church to be counter-cultural, you might try answering the following question? Are not the media advertisers the new elders in the community? Do we doubt that MTV is geared to the identity and intimacy questions of tweens and adolescents? Do we doubt that adults are mightily challenged by celebrities as sources of meaning and purpose in life? Who are the major authorities for most young people?

There are, however, already warning signs that such a trivializing culture is exhausted. The best of today's young people are unsatisfied and long to return to a simpler and a more basic life. Juliette Schorr in *The Overspent American* thinks that twenty percent of the young already seek a simpler, deeper life.

My Three Hopes for the Young

I was thrust into understanding the cultural change going on in the United States of necessity. I had taught high school religion in the 1950s. I left the United States in 1960 for four years of seminary study in Europe and upon returning to the same high school was soon aware that teaching religion to high school seniors now would be quite different. The senior curriculum included three major themes: the theology of the

Church, the Church's social teaching on justice, (particularly poverty, racism and war) and the states of life and vocation (marriage, single life, religious and priestly). From day one I found seniors in my classes much more challenging than they had been in 1960. The Vietnam War was raging, the war on poverty and racial injustice were topics of daily news, the sexual revolution had taken hold, and government and Church were seriously questioned. My seniors were skeptical. Accepting assumptions and values of the past could not be taken for granted. A senior appeared at my house one evening to tell me he had just confronted his parents and said to them "my religion is not your religion." A few days into the semester a student brought me Bob Dylan's album "The Times They Are a Changin" just to let me know that, in case I had any doubt. I met students deeply distressed by Vietnam, who had nightmares about fighting there and others who would become conscientious objectors. There were lots of questions about the failure of institutions to grapple with society's pain. I enjoyed this time in class with seventeen year-olds immensely. These were the questions of the Second Vatican Council itself. I was in a religion lab and both students and teacher found a great deal of vitality in wrestling with the questions. I did a lot of reading and listening those two years. I have remained closer to this group of students than to any I have ever had.

I am not suggesting that we live in continuity with the 1960s but I do believe that a serious disconnect of the young and the Church began there. It was followed by other phases of young people's evolution that we have just not addressed or coped with well. This chapter is about understanding the culture of the young and about finding the resonances between their world and our message.

In all kinds of groups I have worked with from diocesan synods to parish pastoral councils, concern for the young has always emerged as the highest of all priorities. I venture to guess that if the Church were to hold a vast assembly in America that concern for youth and young adults would be far and away the most important national priority. Universally we are concerned, but the hard fact is that we continue to do very little. I explain this to myself in various ways: 1) we don't know quite where to begin; 2) we know that developing any processes would require concentrated research, study and reflection and we tell ourselves we don't have the time; 3) we haven't understood well-enough the cultural shifts since the 1960s and do not know how to engage the growth factors in the culture (e.g., fulfillment and freedom concerns); 4) we are at least preconsciously aware that the sexually repressive image of the Church makes young people difficult candidates for any effort; 5) we don't know any successful models that have produced significant results (although we know "Lifeteen" and "Theology on Tap" offer some promise). I have settled on the belief that all of the above are true in great measure. Ministry to the young may be in our hearts but we are severely stuck on the operational level.

I used to hear that the young who drift away from the church "will return, after they marry and have children." I haven't heard that for some time now. Some few might but far fewer than we imagined years ago. My experience is that most non-practicing, young baptized Catholics move directly into a secular American materialistic lifestyle with limited horizons based on personal comfort; into some sort of religious fundamentalism that banishes most contemporary questions with simplistic answers based on Biblical literalism, or into what sociologist Wade Roof calls the "spiritual marketplace" where one creates one's own religion out of favorite practices for getting in touch with self or the power "up there" (e.g., Zen, meditation, astrology, Chicken Soup books, holistic healing, Sufism, recovery movements, magic and witchcraft). All of the above alternatives seem a great distance from Paul's proclamation and commitment to "Jesus Christ yesterday, today and forever" to which Christians have historically pledged their faith and devotion.

In the last chapter I cited Karl Rahner's insight that "it is not faith that has changed in our time but the world around it." Fellow Jesuit philosopher, Bernard Lonergan, puts the same thought this way: that the contemporary world is undergoing "a crisis not of faith but of culture." Rahner goes quite far when he warns that faith can even risk self-destruction if it fails to create the forms demanded by a new culture that it doesn't understand. The statement of Pope John Paul II in *Centesimus Annus* (p. 86) that we should be involved in discovering the language to reach people in their depth calls out to us now.

I have always enjoyed children. I like to talk to them as they begin to understand the world and use language. They say the most interesting things in very funny ways as they begin to figure things out. I love their uniqueness and the way they unfold before our eyes. I chose to be a high school teacher so that I might spend time and energy to help adolescents continue to find their way on their unique life path and live joyful lives.

When preparing to write this chapter it became clear to me that I had three hopes in my work with teenagers. The first was that they would experience themselves as unique and would develop and value the identity that is innate in them. The second was that they be rooted and founded in love expressed in living the beatitudes. The third hope was, in my first formulation, that they be contemporary people open to the possibilities the world presents in our time. I was much impressed by Teilhard de Chardin's sense that people needed to live in and love the world of their time. It is there that they will find their life, joy and meaning. Christians have always believed that God is active now in working out our history with us. Later, I realized that being contemporary also meant being critically analytic. It is important to remember what St. Paul says to us about the power of evil in our midst—that it is not against human enemies that we have to struggle but "against the Principalities and Powers who originate the darkness of this world." The enemies of Jesus were formidable. Do we think the enemies of true life are any less powerful today? Robert Bly calls them "giants, large and cruel, behind the scenes, lurking just out of sight: a feeling, sexuality and ferocity system."

Consumerism and the Christian Alternative

My first concern as I have said was to help young people come to love their particular, unique being. To realize deeply and enjoy the truth that no one quite like them ever existed before or ever will again grounds the God-given essential self. Memories, hopes, fears, joys, desires, love, abilities are unrepeatable. No one could ever do what they do in the way they do it. We have probably heard some of these things said to us somewhere during our life, probably in a church setting (if anywhere else except family it probably was in some ad to manipulate you into buying something). In our heart of hearts we hope this is all true. It is of the essence of our faith. One of my favorite Baptismal homily themes comes off the statement of St. Augustine: "God loves each one of us as if there were only one of us to love." Each of us is a very particular creation.

In contrast, how about these words from the *New York Times* of April 22, 2007, in an article entitled, "Tweens are Shoppers" by Lesley Jane Seymour, who when shopping with her children "enjoys the fact that they get to select and survey a world of identities and selves that are present out there." I was more than a little uncomfortable with all that. "Out there . . . to survey and select identity." Now that is what I would call a "fall from grace" for someone who might believe that God created each one to be a unique image and likeness and that our task was to discover within just what we were. In Ms. Seymour's model I can shop for one of the available identities offered by advertisers. Samuel Barber, popular writer on consumerism, describes it well as "produced inauthenticity," defining ourselves by what we buy: "Faux values at the core of identity exacts a price." Sociologist Juliet Schor describes it as "brands giving you value and self-esteem as an endless, fruitless, finally depressing enterprise." When she says that this kind of advertising is the dominant transmitter of culture and identity, I shiver. I often think how authentically human are the faces I see among the poor of the world on the evening news. When Juliet Schor says we have produced a generation "that is not very nice" she sounds excessively harsh. Barber sees the same thing and puts it this way "we sow as individuals what we would not necessarily choose to reap as a community" . . . The image of the "cool" young will not do much to save the world.

We have to fight this battle now in all our work with parents and young people. We are fighting for their uniqueness and identity, their vocation and mission in the world. What is on sale in the identity market is below the dignity and meaning of our children and young people.

Economists and sociologists who have seen our world develop over the last fifty years recognize that we are faced with the capitalist dilemma. The earlier quotation from Pope John Paul II on consumerism indicates this creation of false needs. Everywhere today we hear children and adolescents cry, "I need that." However the challenge now is for the capitalist market to grow to meet the real needs of all the people of the world. We have created and continue to create ever more of these needs. The desire is literally endless. Capitalism made a choice: if the poor cannot be enriched enough to become consumers, then people in the richer countries with vast income and sixty percent of the world's consumption already, will have to be enticed into more shopping. Marx called these "imaginary needs" and Freud thought they were "the pathology of cultural communities." The people of the less-developed world, the global majority, still has immense and real needs but the market alone will not respond. Those people don't have any money now. It is into this world of the young that the materialists of our time have entered with full force depriving the young of the larger purpose of their life and communicating that everyone's life consists mainly of acquiring things for oneself. Donald Orr, author of *Ecological Literacy: Education and the Transition to a Post-Modern World,* states it even more strongly; "the consumer economy is a cheat and a fraud. It consumes everything in its path. Including our children's future. It does not—indeed, cannot—meet our most fundamental needs for solace, belonging and authentic meaning."

John Kavanaugh, S.J. in his classic *Following Christ in a Consumer Society* describes two competing life forms in the world: the gospel of personhood and the gospel of commodity. Each provides continuing images for our consciousness. They serve as ultimates and implore us to follow. We need to have our young people see the Christ of the Gospel living and loving people of his world and struggling with and for them. The

Christ of the beatitudes needs room to grow in the life of the young before and during the attempts made to seduce them into commodity living. In your image-watching look for the underlying image of self-satisfied egotists with all the modern toys living a life with no worries, and a small group of friends. Michael Gallagher suggests we might ask young people questions like, "who is imaging your life for you?" "Who is telling you the stories that claim to show reality?" Even twelve-year olds could see what the culture is trying to do to them, if they stand back and reflect.

Granted that we will never quite know ourselves completely until the moment after our death when all will be clear, we can hope that our young people's lives are on the road to their personal selfhood. In a recent book *Revisiting the Idea of Vocation,* John Neafsey, a psychologist at Loyola University, contributes an essay entitled "Psychological Dimensions of the Discernment of Vocation" in which he weaves together the theological and intrapsychic issues involved in a Christian young person's self-understanding. He notes:

1. Both Thomas Merton and D.W.Winnicott, noted developmental psychologist, writing on ego distortion, make a distinction between the true and false self. For Winnicott the false self is built on conformity. In order to cope and survive emotionally, the person develops a kind of inauthentic mask that is motivated by the need to please or adjust or conform to the expectation of others in order to win their acceptance or avoid their rejection. The true self remains hidden, and in extreme cases, perhaps even forgotten or repressed within the unconscious of the person.

2. Vocation, as a universal and archetypal experience has been spoken of through the ages, as a matter of "hearing a voice, of being addressed by a voice." Every human

person can respond to a call and all of us have the potential to hear and follow a voice within us. The call is to be a particular kind of person and to do particular things.

3. The voice of God can be heard through feelings, thoughts, images and dreams of our inner world but also through the significant life events, people and circumstances that we encounter. The purpose of observing and reflecting on these patterns is that they deepen our sense of ourselves and they can show us where, for each one of us, the Spirit of God is leading.

4. The thoughts within us are spoken to us within our mind by God who gives us the thought in order to help us. The true self, or *imago Dei*, emerges in this nurturing, growth-promoting, transformative relationship.

5. In *The Varieties of Religious Experience*, William James refers to this place where psyche and spirit meet as "the wider self" through which saving experiences come. There can be a "new zest which adds itself like a gift to life, a sense of "lyrical enchantment" or "earnestness" or "heroism," an "assurance of safety and a temper of peace" and "a preponderance of loving affections." St. Paul describes these emotional effects of the Holy Spirit on the human person in his Letter to the Galatians: "joy, peace, patience, kindness, goodness, trustfulness, gentleness, and self-control."

6. The meaning and significance of the feelings indicate the direction in which we are moving. The Spirit leads us into a progressive overcoming and surrender of egocentric concerns. The ultimate aim is to live, work and love even more creatively, deeply and freely. Becoming such a person is not easy. It is a call to individuation "becoming what we are" within the unique circumstances of our life.

7. In conclusion, as Parker Palmer, a popular spiritual writer says in *Let Your Life Speak: Listening for the Voice of Vocation,* vocation does not come from willfulness. It comes from listening. I must listen to my life and try to understand what it is truly about . . . vocation does not mean a goal I pursue. It means a calling I hear. This is what the poet knows and what every wisdom tradition teaches: there is a great gulf between the way my ego wants to identify me, with its self-protective masks and self-serving fictions and my true self.

8. There is no blueprint in God's mind with which we have to comply. The discernment of spirits we are describing is within a living relationship with God. Mistakes are part of the bargain; life would not be complete without them. There is no sure road map. We may have to recognize the error of a direction we have taken or an error we have made.

   This sense of personal vocation and discernment of gifts and aptitudes takes us along the path to recognizing the unique participation each person has been given in the drama of the human community.

The second of my concerns: that the young be founded in love and become convinced that a life based on the beatitudes is the path to the fullest life. Jesus explicitly announces that he comes so that we "may have life and have it abundantly." The highest revelation of the path to this life he revealed to us in the beatitudes (Mt 5:3-12):

Blessed are the poor in spirit, for theirs is the kingdom of heaven

Blessed are those who mourn, for they will be comforted.

Blessed are the meek, for they will inherit the earth.

Blessed are those who hunger and thirst for justice, for they will have their fill

Blessed are the merciful, for they will obtain mercy.

Blessed are the pure of heart, for they will see God.

Blessed are the peacemakers, for they will be called children of God.

Blessed are those who are persecuted in the cause of justice, for theirs is the kingdom of heaven.

We need to talk to the young about this as a life-style today. When I think of the people in my life who closely approximate this way of being, they are the most loving and happy people I have ever met. They have their particular ways of being, attentive, responsive, respectful and caring when you are in their presence. I think they must be particularly graced but then I think they must have grown up in an environment that fostered such virtues. Then I remind myself of a few people I know who have had difficult and heartbreaking family histories hidden away and still manage to seem so graced. Whatever the story each has, I always feel privileged to meet a person who lives the beatitudes.

A useful exercise I have adapted from David Walsh and used with both parents and young people of all ages is to take the concepts of "success," "fulfillment" and "freedom," create two columns, "Meaning in the contemporary marketplace" and "Meaning in the Christian family" and have them tell me what these words mean in both worlds. The contrast is very clear and the participants see what a great chasm there is between these two worlds.

Walter Bruggemann gives a beautiful description of the work we need to do with young people in the Church. In chapter four of *Biblical Perspectives on Evangelization*, "Beloved Children Become Belief-ful Adults," he sketches out why it is necessary to face up to the challenge of confronting the cultures to which our children are constantly exposed.

For Bruggemann evangelization is not just a program strategy but the enactment of the hope and energy of the community. The core stories of Scripture enable us to see the shallowness of the stories we may have embraced from the surrounding culture. It invites us to "switch stories" and therefore to re-imagine our lives.

For Bruggeman there is always a massive and hidden struggle for the shape and governance of the world. God entered the combat in the coming of Jesus to the poor. But it will not just be Jesus who will have to struggle. In prosperity we can get amnesia; affluence easily drives out gratitude. Jeremiah 2:1-13 reminds us that we are tempted to trade Jehovah for something contemporary, cheap, quick, and trivial.

Bruggemann feels deeply that the task of evangelization of the young is enormously urgent for us now. Nurture and incorporation into faith are not so easy for our children. They require ongoing conversation so that a little bit at a time the child claims the "news" that defines us. The conversation itself is the reality of evangelization. Our children are easily seduced into the comfortable life. Acquisitiveness, greed and indifference to others are almost "marching orders." It is not a question of major conversations but one, which connects the "little pieces" of daily life to the larger context of faith. We can help create "a community of girls and boys with vision and little ones who are not so trapped." The community of the Church has not convinced the young of the power and validity of the Gospel—that the free market is not an adequate framework on which to build a viable human community.

As I indicated at the beginning of this chapter we are in many ways struggling with our young people as Augustine struggled with his acceptance of Christianity.

While writing this chapter I ran across a talk given by Archbishop Diarmud Martin of Dublin who was addressing seminarians on "how to present the gospel to a younger generation." It struck me that five of his remarks could frame a discussion for leaders in churches.

1. Ministry in the future "will certainly not be 'business as usual.' " People will be coming from a wide variety of starting points. Their path will take you to a world where many of the traditional prerequisites for belonging to the Church will no longer be relevant ones. Young people will come having very little of the traditional knowledge and culture of their faith.

2. We should not be dreaming of a golden age of the past, of a religious culture that is no longer there. Faith can take root if we help believers discern the superficialilities and overcome some of the forces of individualism, which can dominate them today.

3. The coming generation has the possibility of encountering Jesus in a context where they are free from traditional narrowness. It can allow the perennial newness of the Gospel to change people in a way that was less possible in the past.

4. Jesus addresses us in a special language and in our work of evangelization we have to use that same language. Asked what Jesus' language was Archbishop Martin answered, "it is the language of healing and the restoration of people to their fullness in freedom."

5. Jesus' message is above all an encounter with a person who addresses us in our history, in our lives. If a liberating personal encounter with Jesus hasn't happened then we have not understood what Christianity is about.

The Archbishop concluded by asking his audience whether in a world searching for wholeness, for deeper roots upon which to construct its values and its future, the churches are making their best contribution in an effective way.

These five statements are bold and hopeful statements for our time. We need to study and engage them in dialogue with those interested in speaking to the next generation. They are emancipatory of defensiveness and could free us for new approaches to the young.

In some recent research Christian Smith, Chairperson of the Sociology Department of the University of North Carolina speaks of teenagers espousing some kind of "benign whateverism" as their religious form. It's composed of some generalized morality, devotional services and a church piety somewhat removed from their daily life. Again, a far cry from Paul's call to "Jesus Christ yesterday, today and forever." Going beyond his sociological findings Smith talks about the need for adults, especially parents to be engaged. He would suggest that we need to see our youth involvement with the Church as a largely family ministry concern. Many adults seem to be intimidated by teenagers and are afraid of being seen as "uncool." He also sees the need to challenge the assumptions of the young. Too many parents see religion as "church-is-good-because-it-will-keep-my-kid-off drugs-and-increase-their- seat-belt-use" mentality. The instrumentalist, "producing healthy and good citizens instead of committed believers" reduces religion to being useful in achieving personal goals.

Smith finds that many teenagers "can feel happy being part of a tradition they were raised in, which to them feels largely satisfactory even if not terribly central or important." Many young people "were comfortable talking about God but not specifically about Jesus." We have to deal with the fact that the youth formation table is dominated structurally by more powerful and vocal actors. Teenagers know about television characters and pop stars, but are quite vague about Moses and Jesus. Smith's research clearly indicates the vast gap between what can pass for religion and the life committed to Christ.

The Reflections of Charles Taylor

The most creative efforts to enter the world of young today, I have found in the work of Charles Taylor. *Sources of the Self*, mentioned earlier, is a classic study of how modern people understand themselves. Taylor offers a most humane analysis of how we got to where we are historically in our understanding of what it means to be a person, a self, and a human agent. Two of his other books *The Ethics of Authenticity* and *A Catholic Modernity* are filled with insight into the modern psyche. Yankelovich, in the 60s spoke of "approaching young people reverently and helping them elevate their sense of the sacred and expressive side of life." Taylor is sensitive to that task as we discern with him the signs of readiness for religion and the revelation made in Jesus within a modern context. There are eight of these signs that I have discerned in Taylor's writing.

I would propose the following eight themes about modernity as "entry points" for constructing an approach to the young. I suggest you sit with them, and reflect and talk to thoughtful young people about them. Each of these themes has had a time and place in Christian spirituality. A few would be the very spirit of the early Church and are certainly scriptural in origin. Others have been appreciated only recently; some have been ignored and feared for many centuries. They can all be embraced as truly Catholic. I take seriously his challenge in *The Ethics of Authenticity;* "what we need to explain is what is peculiar to our time." Not to do this loses the power of the ideal of authenticity.

The eight themes are:

1. The affirmation of daily life
2. Inwardness as a basis for spirituality
3. The expression of romance
4. The celebration of nature
5. The freedom and the desire to be oneself
6. The dedication to reduce human suffering
7. The affirmation of universal human rights
8. A personal relationship to a transcendent God

1. **The affirmation of daily life.** This is Taylor's most recurrent theme. Throughout history there has been a tendency towards division into higher and lower: rich and poor, citizen and non-citizen, holy ones, nobles, and "common people." Contemplation for the Greeks was higher than action. The Church spoke of the sacred and the profane. In the 18th century the ideal of equality and the rights of man had emerged in western consciousness to the point of beginning to eliminate distinctions among people because of birth and class. We continue to try to break down distinctions in our time by eliminating racial, ethnic, and religious barriers. Taylor concludes: "what is important for my purpose is this positive side, the affirmation that the fullness of Christian existence was to be found within the activities of this life, in one's calling and in marriage and family. As N.T. Wright says in *The Challenge of Jesus*: "The key thing was that the inbreaking kingdom of Jesus was announcing a new world, a new context, and He was challenging His hearers to become the new people that this context demanded. He was offering a challenge to His contemporaries to a way of life, a way of forgiveness and prayer, a way of

jubilee, which they could practice in their own villages, right where they were." God was always present in fullness in the ordinary places of the world. All life is hallowed and all are beloved. He promised the possibility of abundant life to every person, a fountain within fed by the Spirit in the ordinary circumstances of life.

2. **Inwardness as a basis for spirituality.** We live in a fast and busy culture. We have many distractions and much to entertain us. However, the signs of cultural exhaustion are all around: trivialization, boredom and depression have never been so widespread. As I indicated earlier, Juliet Schor sees a full 20% of young people who want a simple, more basic life; they are thoughtful, sensitive bearers of good news for people today. They are attracted to silence and wonder, heart-listening, personal prayer and contemplation and deeper friendships. They understand the spirituality of their work. They know about the inner space where I may speak to my Creator as Augustine did. It is in my distinctive inwardness that my life can be a work of art. Not to do so leaves one in a world of superficial conformity, which occludes the deeper meanings of life and makes them hard to discern.

3. **The expression of romance.** Sexuality certainly has been a Catholic tension over the years. Out of fear of a pagan world's abuse of women (seen in Paul) and in Augustine's fear of the power of sin in sexual expression we have been defensive for centuries. John Paul II tried to deal with these issues in his extensive writings on the value and beauty of the human body.

Over the past fifty years I have seen the fruits of the rise of romance in the time in which we now live. I can see it often on the streets of New York where I live, in the air of gentle, affectionate and erotic display. Young people look like they are relating as equals and in role-free ways. In the best young people I see men who look less macho, less demanding, less in charge. Women are more self-sufficient, independent and confident. New meeting ground is available.

Someone I read years ago thought that when we look back on the 20th century that the single most notable event will have been the emancipation of women in society. In other words, give women more equality and freedom and you may have an increased possibility for healthier love relationships.

Andrew Greeley has written much about beauty, charm and the Church in recent years that is helpful for us. In an article entitled "Catholicism and Beauty," he encourages us to remember that beauty is primary. It overwhelms us, enchants us, fascinates us, and calls us. "We are stopped in our tracks and then drenched in luminosity by an encounter with beauty." This is never truer than when "falling in love." We need to talk about this more in the Church.

Although guilt and gloom about sex have just about disappeared in my lifetime, stupidity about sex can be rampant among those with little foundation in empathy. It is wonderful and a marvel for someone to be deeply in love. The beloved other knows us, desires us passionately and wants to be one in mind and heart. True equality enhances love. One of the most rewarding experiences I have had was as facilitator of a post-Cana group for those married within the last two years. It is an obvious innovation that most churches should consider.

4. **The celebration of nature.** The pagan world into which Christianity moved in the first century was filled with the worship of gods of natural forces: gods of forest, sea and sky, gods of the under and upper worlds. Into this pagan world the revelation of the one true God became the center of Jewish faith. In subsequent history Jews and Christians would demythologize nature and place emphasis on this one God and relationship to

the human community as sacred. Nature was emptied of its pagan mystery. From the fourth century onward "nature" fell into decline. Invasions, wars, disease and death dominated much of human consciousness in Europe. It would only be in the eighteenth century that "nature" would again become central. Jean Jacques Rousseau became the great apostle of the beauty of nature and the natural. Taylor sees this rebirth "like a homecoming to a garden." He sees Rousseau to be at the starting point of a transformation in modern culture. Rousseau felt the call to open ourselves to the élan of nature without and within. Nature is wondrous. It deposes egoism and utilitarianism and resonates with our deeper nature, our freedom and our appreciation of the everyday.

The children of Rousseau are all over the world today. This aspect of the celebration of nature is an area we need to "recognize and retrieve." The fullness of the earth is a reminder of the wonder in which we live. The strong thrust among the young today to save the planet is truly a spiritual and religious concern.

5. **Freedom and the desire to be oneself.** We have spoken of this theme throughout this whole chapter. We are freer today to live out our identity, but there are still many children in our society deprived of the opportunity to develop because of poverty, racism and a dysfunctional family life. Many of the more advantaged young people feel the responsibility to work for the freedoms of those less fortunate. And as we have seen in this chapter the young in our society who are the victims of consumer culture also need to be rescued.

Taylor emphasizes what he calls "together goods" in his explanation of this freedom. He mentions conversation, dance, love, friendship, governing oneself, and preaching as "together goods." It is not as though human nature is complete in each one of us. It is much more our potentiality to play our part in "a certain kind of dance." Human life is something that happens between people as the fullness of divine life passes between persons. Taylor will finally locate authentic freedom in what he calls "horizons of significance." I do not determine significance. "Only if I exist in a world in which human history, the demands of nature, the needs of my fellow human beings, the duties of citizenship, or the call of God, or something else of this order matters crucially, can I have an identity for myself that is not trivial."

6. **The dedication to reduce human suffering.** We don't accept that people continue to be potential victims of natural or man-made disasters. We imagine that most of them are preventable or curable. Whether it is hurricanes or famines, sexual abuse or war, poverty or racism, we can and ought to do something. Young people have a strong sense that others should not have to face unnecessary evil in life. Psychologists today tell us that empathy is created within us before we are eight years old and it is derived from our association with empathetic others. In chapter 25 of Matthew's gospel Jesus makes salvation of all nations and persons rest on whatever you do to the least of my brethren: the hungry, the thirsty, strangers, the naked, the sick, prisoners. Many young people today are ready to participate in this salvific effort in their communities.

7. **The affirmation of universal human rights.** It has been a long climb in human history to arrive where we are at this point in western society. Just as young people do not accept suffering as a fact of life, they easily affirm the universal rights of every person. Taylor puts it this way "we are called today to stretch out so far, so consistently, so systematically, so as a matter of course, to the stranger outside the gate." However, he warns us against the anger he has seen in those who fight for

human rights. He sees it often in the efforts of modern secular humanists, which are often, not rooted deeply enough in love. He sees the right's culture often stuck on "what can be established by law quite apart from the moral responsibility of the community." Taylor concludes: "the very idea of expressing basic human norms in terms of rights already nudges us away from understanding Christian responsibility." As Christians we have the very motivation of God to persist in what are often long and very difficult struggles.

8. **A personal relationship to a transcendent God.** Over the years talking with young people who have become agnostics, I am often disappointed in their understanding of a God who may exist as something like "a power," "a force of the universe." After all, if the most sublime experience is the personal dimension and human love, why couldn't God qualify to be at least as much a person as we are.

In any case there will come a time in everyone's life when the religious question becomes relevant. Research shows that it tends to arise out of the major positive and negative experiences of life. I find the research of Leon McKenzie and Matt Hayes very helpful in thinking about dialogue with young people.

Mackenzie and Hayes investigated what strengthening and weakening experiences had affected adult faith. The following, in order of frequency, were the strengthening faith experiences:

1. Faith strengthened through a painful event (such as illness or death of family members or friends). It is interesting that painful events are the first mentioned as both strengthening and weakening experiences.
2. Prayers answered (e.g., health restored or things avoided)
3. Parenting (involving awe over children, concern for their upbringing in faith and sacramental events in their lives)

4. Home and neighborhood environment (mostly witnessing attitudes of parents, grandparents and peers in daily life)

5. Renewal experiences (various programs of personal and parish renewal)

6. Marriage (relationship to a spouse as influential in faith development)

7. Institutional (Catholic education, relationship with a priest, reception of the sacraments)

The weakening of faith experiences in the order of frequency were:

1. "Why" experiences (questioning God about illness or death, the presence of injustice in the world)

2. Church leadership (harsh personal treatment by priests, religious sisters or brothers, negative experiences with Catholic education)

3. Uncomfortableness with the changing Church (perceived changing standards of right and wrong, change in long-standing practices)

4. Lack of change in the Church (this institutional element singled out the Church's practice on divorce and remarriage and its teaching on birth control)

5. Home and neighborhood environment (peer group influences, changing social trends and family atmosphere)

6. Hypocrisy among believers (the failure to practice what is essential to the gospel among church-going people)

Of course, from what we have been saying about the effect of consumer society on young people, a resultant inner distraction from the deeper questions of life can eliminate religious questions for a long time and easily lead to a general avoidance of religious questions in general. Taylor, in a telling phrase finds that the young have been brought up in an environment "inhospitable to the transcendent . . . as if there were nothing beyond—more, as though it weren't a crying need of the human heart to open that window, gaze and then go beyond; as though feeling this need were the result of a mistake, an erroneous world view, bad conditioning or worse, some pathology."

As I thought about Taylor's observations I was reminded of the provocative work of John Meagher in his *The Truing of Christianity:*

The leaders of the Christian churches have normally insisted on loyalty to what Christianity has been, with relatively little attention to what Christianity can become. Our responsibility includes assisting it to change, some-times to retreat as well as to advance, to learn new ways of life and thought, to live more appropriately in order to live more abundantly and to think more critically in order to think more truly. We will fail our great-grandchildren if we pass on to them only what we have received . . . There is much more Christianity ought to be that it has not yet become; there is much that it has been that will no longer do.

Michael Gallagher's university students who were seeking to be Catholics today also put it quite well. They wanted:

1. to be true to their time
2. to be honest about their struggles
3. to seek out communities of faith support
4. to pursue an education that would give them hope for future faith development
5. to find ways of praying more deeply
6. to discover outlets into active social involvement

A Working Process: Holy Family Parish

To conclude this chapter, I would like to describe the effort of Father Patrick Brennan to work with youth and young adults in his parish, Holy Family, in Inverness, Illinois. Brennan had spent many years as Director of Catholic Evangelization in the Archdiocese of Chicago. His early book, *The Evangelizing Parish* had described his first efforts to develop a program for evangelizing the young. In 2007 he published *The Mission-Driven Parish* about the work he has been developing recently. He describes parishes that have varied programs for the young: socially orientated teen clubs, religious education programs, retreat programs, and volunteer programs. However, few offer a full-range of opportunities for young people to develop as Christians. We know the right pieces; we just need to structure them in a meaningful way.

He builds his approach on the importance of "moral conversations" (a term borrowed from the psychiatrist Robert Coles). All of us grow by having moral conversations, especially with trusted mentors. The absence of these conversations result in stunted development. Erickson, Coles and others remind us of the uniquely spiritual nature of adolescence. They are not religious in organized, institutional ways but they develop the mental ability to deal with the moral and spiritual issues that confront them. At this point of development "parish churches offer little or nothing to help adolescents grow as disciples of Jesus Christ." Brennan developed a program that he called F.L.A.M.E., (friendship, leadership, acceptance, ministry, and education). Rather than summarize in detail here, I refer you to chapter nine of *The Mission Driven Parish* for a more complete description of the processes involved. He has created retreat experiences, inter-generational small Christian communities, follow-up to the sacrament of confirmation, and the

Kairos model for older teens. There is a special group to plan social events and large and small group educational events.

Young adults are quickly invited into ministry and service organizations. Worship services are specially geared to young adults. He has also experimented with non-Eucharistic worship services presided over by young adults. There are follow-up meetings for all those married 1-5 years. At the present time there are about seven hundred young people involved in youth and young adult ministry at Holy Family. This is about one-third of the number of young in the parish. In its five-year plan Holy Family resolved in one of its goals "to dramatically improve efforts to evangelize youth in the next two to five years." In its young adult ministry efforts there are commitments to "increase the number of un-churched invited into the R.C.I.A. program by 25 percent each year in the next five years."

I am naïve enough to believe that local parish churches are the only places where local community and non-consumerist society can be rebuilt, especially for the young.

The following chapters offer us hope for synergy among those called to build parish life, a model for planning and a whole new way of working toward a parish where responsibility is widely dispersed. The task of creating a truly active modern Church is far from easy but it is challenging to us and important to Christ. Wade Roof tells us that the religious question the young are asking is: "Is this a place or person that can nourish me?" Let us hope it is.

5

Synergy and "Great Groups" in Parish Life

⊘∿∿⊘

IN this chapter I would like to describe the dynamics that can result from groups working well together in parish life. I no longer am inspired by stories of what one outstanding pastor can do to vitalize a parish because of his energy, personal vision and commitment. Books like *Excellent Catholic Parishes* serve their purpose in giving us examples of innovation. However, they are not widely imitable because of the super-human energy of the pastor involved. I find it more helpful to think of a few parishes I know where the pastor is inspired and committed but of average energy and where his real charisms are discerning the giftedness of parishioners and the creation of structures where people work well together. I have long subscribed to Peter Drucker's famous axiom about good managers—"good managers get above average performance out of average people."

In this chapter I would like to reflect on two helpful concepts found in organizational literature in recent years—synergy and "great group" theory. Synergy is not a word I hear in the Church. To be perfectly honest I have found that managing conflict or managing differences is the main part of my work with groups. Many church groups are satisfied with "just getting along" where differences are avoided and people have their own turf. Finding communities where members appreciate the gifts of others and attempt almost naturally to listen carefully to others' viewpoints and truly become interdependent is rather rare in my experience. I can see it in married couples who grow more understanding and in families that are close. I have found it to a higher degree in two places in my work in the Church: ad hoc groups and among high-performing humble people (we will return to this theme soon).

Webster defines synergy as "the combined healthy action of every organ of a particular system." It seems that in general, things go remarkably well synergistically in the biological world. We have more difficulties as we go up the human scale of emotion, love, and life together in communities, nations and the world. We are told in the first chapter of Genesis that we are images of God. Social evolution is the task of our time. Working together synergistically is the hope of God; God for us. Going it alone doesn't look like the style of the Creator.

I don't think I am naïve as a Christian to have high hopes for synergy. I believe that whenever there is a creative spirit in an individual or group, the Holy Spirit is operative. Jesus tells us "that whatever is born of the Spirit is the Spirit" (Jn 3: 6). Paul reminds us that we are called to serve "in the newness of spirit" and that "the spirit gives testimony to our spirit." In any good work we undertake we should expect that the Spirit will be "creating" with us. As a practical guideline I am inclined to think that groups need about a year (or about eight to ten meetings) to thoughtfully understand an issue, get perspective on it as it applies to the local scene, and do background research by reading and finding others locally and nationally who have already done good work in the area. Goals and strategies need to follow deep understandings. One day at a meeting I attended that was rushing toward premature solutions the old Latin proverb "make haste slowly" suddenly came to mind. We need not rush the planning of a major effort.

The second suggestion I would make is to follow the advice of Jim Collins in *Good to Great* when he advises:

1. Get the right people on the bus, the wrong people off the bus, and the right people in the right seats.
2. Figure out where to drive it together.
3. Confront the brutal facts and never lose faith.
4. Remember that there is no defining action, no grand program and no miracle moment.

Collins challenges the usual thinking about beginning with "what" you want to do and then finding "who" will do it. He imagines that a pool of talented people will determine "where the bus ought to go" better than any individual leader might do. With the right people, the problem of both motivation and management largely goes away. The first step in getting the right people on the bus is the spiritual discernment of gifts. More ingenuity may be required to get the wrong people off the bus. I have no easy answer for how to do that except to believe that all people have charisms and some people are not in the area of charism where they can contribute most. For whatever ministry we consider specific gifts are needed. For any ministry I think we can narrow down the major qualities and skills to about five. Finding the members for a working group is much easier when these characteristics are clear. I have even had people disqualify themselves when they saw the final list of qualities needed, e.g., patience and creativity as qualities for a parish council member. Well-discerned groups on such issues as those of lay leadership, evangelization and youth work or any other ministry will figure out where to drive the bus. These groups will have to "confront the brutal facts and never lose faith." My experience is that well-chosen groups are willing to do that. Such people are highly committed to doing the imaginative work required. In fact, they rather enjoy the struggle and the challenge. Collins describes such leaders as marked by two characteristics: extreme personal humility and intense professional will. Such people have "fierce resolve to do whatever is needed to make the company great" but "their ambition is first and foremost for the institution, not themselves." They are sustained by what they are building and the hope for what will be lasting and excellent.

Overcoming Obstacles and Resistance

Often groups get bogged down early by "obstacles" that individuals raise at meetings. At start-up time I remind the group that obstacles are just that. They are things in the way. They need to be avoided, overcome, finessed, dealt with. There are bound to be obstacles and differences of perspective in any work we undertake together. We must go forward and not allow "obstacles" to prevent movement.

Recent research indicates that about 19% of executives are skeptics. In the general population the number gets as high as 50%. I frequently ask groups to accept the norm established by Jack Welch when he was CEO of General Electric: "we are here to expand and enrich *all* ideas." He wanted to get beyond a pro and con culture. William Lynch, S.J., put it very well years ago in his fine work, *The Integrating Mind*: "either/or thinking is the curse of the American mind." My request to people is that differences be pointed out in the framework of "enriching and enhancing. As Catholics we have the added curse of all large institutions that "nay-sayers" have more power than "yea-sayers." I very often see groups in a discussion raise a few points, begin a pro and con discussion, and get stuck. Élan is stifled because of too much "obstacle" thinking.

A key experience for me many years ago took place at a meeting of the diocesan staff of Catholic Charities in the diocese of Rockville Centre. The director, a most capable leader, chaired the meeting. There were a number of subcommittee reports each followed by a lively and focused group discussion among the forty or so participants. The group accepted or improved the recommendations of the subcommittees. This meeting became a paradigmatic experience for me. I had witnessed an excellent meeting. It surely explains some of my enduring faith in the possibility of vital and productive meetings. Steven Covey tells us that many people have never been at a truly synergistic meeting and so come to meetings expecting little from themselves or others.

The most successful meetings I ever facilitated were a group of ten or so meetings of a task force on lay ministry in the diocese of Rockville Centre. The group did a great amount of work in and outside of the meetings and within ninety days had gone from data gathering about lay ministry in the diocese to recommending a new Institute of Pastoral Formation. We consulted nationally and did a thorough consultation with all ministries within the diocese on existing ministry training programs. All committee members had full-time jobs, while doing this. But the energy for the task was so high it never seemed to be a burden for them. Within seven months we had gone from evaluating existing programs to implementing curriculum, selecting staff, and advertising a September opening.

Creativity in the System

The Trinity is the great archetype of all synergy. We believe that there have always been three Eternal Persons who understood each other and loved each other infinitely. Their inner world is one of shared creativity and goodness. The created world in which we live reflects this synergistic dynamic when it is in process of fulfilling its destiny. The Trinity created a wholly synergistic universe. We recognize our eco-system filled with untold diversity and possibility for development (by itself and with human discoveries uncovering the relationships among things—think only of our participation in the development of pharmaceuticals or space exploration and even poetry). The human body is a system filled with complex sub-systems meant to work harmoniously and in service to the whole body. The family reflects this same synergistic design of the Creator God. The Church (it is clear in Paul) has this same oneness of purpose and diversity of function—to be one Body. We need to look for synergy and create synergy in our relationships and groups if we would reflect Trinitarian life.

When speaking about synergy we often hear that in social interactions, 1+1=3. Two people in interdependence can achieve more than two people alone. In groups that I have facilitated, members often do their own reflection on issues, but when the group assembles, associations are made that no one had made privately. When we talk so much about collaboration today, it should be clear that the primary outcome of collaboration is synergy. (In fact, the Greek *synergois* is the New Testament word for "collaborators.") Collaboration may help us avoid duplication; it may be a support to us in our work. But those are by-products of the energy possible when people gather. When Covey says: "synergy works; it is a correct principle," he is close to recognizing the innate order in which the Trinity established the world. Covey continues: "it is the call to be ready for openness, wonder, empathy, humility, sensitivity, the ability to 'let go', tolerance of ambiguity and the spirit of adventure." This seems to be a fairly good list to measure ourselves by as group members.

In listing the blocks to synergy we can name our own genetic makeup which leads us to value particular ways of approaching reality; our natural defensiveness and protection of self which is related to our need for identity; our pride. The valuing of differences is the essence of synergy. We are meant to be complementary. We have "need of each other" as Paul describes in 1 Corinthians. Covey gives two clues for growth in synergistic thinking: "overcoming the master-minding tendency." No one of us has the answer on most things. The second he encourages is to "fish for alternatives." There are multitudes of possibilities for successful solutions. Fishermen need to be both patient and circumspect about their environment.

I conclude these reflections on synergy with some thoughtful observations from Abraham Maslow about synergistic thinking in individuals and organizations. They would serve well for both individual and group reflection.

1. What improves a human being at any point tends to improve the whole human being.

2. Any increase in intrapsychic synergy in any one person is simultaneously a move in the direction of increased synergy in other persons and also in the direction of increased synergy in the team, the organization and society.

3. Any move towards social synergy is also thereby a move toward enlightened management policy, enlightened managers, enlightened workers, enlightened organizations.

4. The better the group is, the more it tends to improve the person within the group. The more this group improves,

the more society improves. Every person's behavior is either a psychotherapeutic or a psycho-pathogenic influence.

5. Self-vitalizing people get pleasure from the pleasure of other people.

6. The ability of people to increase in influence increases the influence pie. Other people's growth in influence does not diminish the influence of supervisors. The more influence and power you give to someone else in the team or organization, the more that is available for all.

7. Synergy is more holistic and more holistic is synergistic.

8. The more teamwork, the more synergy.

9. We must learn to thrill with pride, to get excited, to have a strengthened feeling of accomplishment when one particular little reform or improvement takes place in which we had a part.

10. A multitude of little steps, little committee meetings and little conversations are necessary. Each of these little steps is absolutely necessary and each of them is doing a big job.

Synergistic groups can become great groups. In fact that is the very definition of a great group—one filled with synergy. Warren Bennis, perhaps the most important writer on leadership in recent years, wrote *Organizational Genius* in 1997. He had come to realize that "the usual way of looking at groups and leadership, as separate phenomenon, was no longer adequate. The most exciting groups resulted from a respectful marriage between an able leader and an assemblage of extraordinary people." He began studies on what he came to call "the great group." I have chosen six of his observations about "great groups" because of the particular relevance to our work together in parish groups.

The six truths of Bennis are:

Truth 1: Leaders of great groups love the talent of others and know where to find it. My experience as both a high school guidance director and as facilitator of gift discernment workshops has been an amazing revelation of the gifts of others. I remember leading gift discernment workshops with three successive groups in a parish in three weekends. It was exciting to hear the discoveries made by participants and staff during these days. As I described in chapter one, gift discernment can open up a parish's leadership pool and create excitement. I remember a woman coming to ask me if I thought she would be a good candidate to begin a divorced and separated ministry in the parish. In the instrument I used she had scored highly in discernment, mercy and helping. What was there to say! There she was, a gift of the Spirit in front of me.

Bennis speaks of the leaders in an organization building great groups as a maestro organizing the genius of others. "Recruiting the most talented people possible is the first task of anyone who hopes to create a great group." But equally as true is his observation that "talented people smell out places that are full of promise and energy, places where the future is being made." Original minds see things differently and word of mouth will draw talent. I always trust that the Holy Spirit sends to each community all that it needs to be vital Church. The Catholic Church needs very badly to lift its limited sights at the local level to discover the richness of the gifts of its members.

Truth 2: Great groups are full of talented people who can work together. Both elements, talents and the ability to work together, are important for us today. Most church leaders have found some talented people but Bennis speaks of "being full of talented people." The "working together" is a complex task that demands a structure such as we describe in the next chapter and some good interpersonal and group skills described in chapter one in Sherry Wedell's model for lay leadership formation.

When I was facilitating diocesan parish council training sessions I would always ask at the very beginning of the session if anyone had received any education in their workplace on systematic planning processes and who had received any facilitator training. The numbers were usually 1/3 for planning and 1/2 for facilitator training. It would be wise to ask such questions at the beginning of a group. I have also gone on a search of the general congregation for those skills and have found facilitators for parish councils from within the congregation. Well-educated group leaders provide on-the-job training for groups working together by modeling good group skills. I was asked to do a video for faith-sharing groups by Paulist Press about ten years ago. I was given a 40-minute time frame. I remember sorting through my brain for the essential areas group leaders ought to know about. I came up with four segments: the stages of group growth, the ability to ask open-ended questions, dealing with difficult moments, dealing with difficult people. The first two segments were structure concerns; the last two were interpersonal and group-skill concerns.

Bennis concludes that great groups are work focused. It is not a question of amiability, pleasantness or friendship; he also found that members of great groups are tolerant of personal idiosyncrasies. The task is the social lubricant.

Truth 3: Great groups think they are on a mission from God. We do have the edge here. We know we are on a mission from God when we are attending to the important needs of the

Gospel. It is vital and holy work. "For to you has been given the kingdom"(Lk 6: 20). As Paul tells us "we hold a treasure," albeit "in frail vessels"(2 Cor 4: 7). We have received the mandate of Jesus Himself, "Go therefore into the whole world" and that wonderful line in scripture directed to the disciples as they were "still staring into the sky" after the ascending of Jesus: "Why, men of Galilee, do you stand looking into the sky?" The great promise of the New Testament is that we do work with God in the Holy Spirit. People who work at the tasks of the gospel ought to realize that they are doing something monumental. This powerful vision of being on a mission from God can make even that part of our work that may seem like drudgery or failure, part of the sacrifice required of us.

Truth 4: Great groups see themselves as winning underdogs. We are underdogs at this time in American culture. We have the recent sexual abuse scandals hanging over us. We have a diminishing number of priests (seen as a sign of decline). Our church culture is pictured as authoritarian and dogmatic in a society valuing democracy, freedom for the individual, pluralism and tolerance. As Catholic "insiders" know, our parish experience is quite different; it is life giving for us. At the same time American culture is in death-throes of its own. As a reviewer of *Consumed*, a recent book by Benjamin Barber puts it: "Hollywood movies are cartoonish and trashy; kids reared on video games and fast food miss out on childhood's meaningful pleasures; life at the mall is soulless, much of popular culture is dreck. Today's consumerist economy sustains profitability by creating needs, convincing us that wiis and i phones are necessary. We promote an ethos of infantilization, a mind set of 'induced childishness' in which adults pursue adolescent life-styles." One might be tempted to say that not to be chic in such a culture is a large compliment.

I think the research on the Millenials (those born between 1982-2004) indicates that they already realize much of the emptiness of the appeal of American mass culture. Anyone seriously interested in this generational difference should look at the works of William Strauss and Neil Howe (I found *The Fourth Turning* the most helpful of their books). Juliet Schor in two of her books *The Overworked American* and the *Overspent American* point to the rise of some new awareness about the attractiveness of simpler, more humanly based life-styles. Fairly soon we could be looking very good to the young adults —if we learn how to speak and know what to do. As Brennan points out in *The Mission Based Parish,* a trans-denominational association of churches such as the Willow Creek Association (about 12,000 networked churches throughout the world) have learned how to do inculturation well and use contemporary, popular culture to share it in relevant, life-changing ways with this age group.

In summary, if we are to emerge as a vibrant Church we need to recognize vibrant churches in America now. It would be, as Bennis says a time in which a "feisty David is hurling fresh ideas at a big backward looking Goliath."

Truth 5: Great groups have the right people in the right job. This is Collins' principle of having people in the right seat on the bus. It is a discernment question for both leadership and members. Self-starters find their own way by their own initiative. The rest of us (about 85%) need encouragement, mentoring, coaching, challenge and support to keep moving along our gift path. Sometimes because our brains follow well-worn grooves we become rather unimaginative. I remember working with a relatively proactive staff and heard their evident dissatisfaction with the quality of lectors. They had been stuck on this for some months. Convinced that I did not want to add more work to the core staff, I asked innocently: "Is there anyone in the parish with any special expertise in any allied area?" Immediately a number of the staff members told me about the chairperson of a Speech department at a local college. He was well known to the staff. Why hadn't they thought about enlisting him to assist, if not be responsible for an improved quality of the Liturgy of the Word? Grooved brains. Because we think "staff" or the "usual volunteers" we get badly stuck. A whole new sense needs to be born about discovering our people. Alongside the myth enunciated earlier that the Holy Spirit sends us who we need to do the work of the church locally, I have another collateral myth I adopted from something I read many years ago. It goes something like this: "no matter how good I think I can do this, someone nearby can do it better." That both relieves me and pushes me to explore. I invite you to do the same.

Truth 6: Great groups are their own reward. People love to be in great groups. There is the joy of accomplishment, discovery, creativity and synergy. As I said earlier most people report that they have never been in a great group and therefore have come to tolerate a deadening ordinariness far below what should be expected. Those who know the experience tell us the reward is not money or glory but the creative process itself. As Bennis says "people ache to do good work." If this isn't true for everyone we work with in groups then they may be the wrong people on the bus. Jim Collins encourages us "only do those things we can get passionate about." People who have been in great groups don't forget them even though they may not last very long. Ad hoc groups seem to be most effective at producing results because of their focus and the time limit on the task.

Let me conclude this chapter by indicating Bennis' signs of empowerment in a group. They are implicit in what we have said during this chapter. He gives four:

The first is SIGNIFICANCE, the understanding that what we are doing makes a difference both for the work and the organization. The feeling that we are an active center of the social order and near to the heart of things, gives group members a sense of profound meaning.

The second characteristic, COMPETENCY, comes from the sense that the group is developing and learning on the job. Work for such groups is post-graduate education. There is a sense of mastery and even new horizons.

The third characteristic is a growing sense of COMMU-NITY; we are joined in a common purpose. We rely on each other because of a common purpose. Bennis quotes an executive at Intel saying: "It is that occasional epiphany which occurs when an exquisitely complicated effort is coordinated and completed well."

The fourth aspect is ENJOYMENT or just plain fun. The intensity sometimes becomes giddiness. That everything is potentially enjoyable is a Bennis' thesis, and an excellent one to trust.

6

A Systematic Planning Model

ᘯᕮᕽᘯᕮᕽ

A THEME frequently mentioned throughout these pages has been the need to plan systematically as your group explores possibilities for action on major parish initiatives.

In recent years when I have done workshops on "How To Run a Meeting," I always start with asking the group to help me make a list of "good meeting—bad meeting" characteristics. The lists I get are just about identical each time. On the "bad meeting" list, themes like "wandering, aimlessness, and randomness" comprise about half of the comments; the other half describes insensitive people in terms like "one-issue people, the know-it-all, bomb throwers, those who talk too much." The "good meeting" list is the converse of the bad: "well planned, moving toward goals, has momentum, is well facilitated." However, there are almost no references to "good behavior" on the part of members. It seems that good behavior is taken for granted. Almost no one says that "people are understanding, manage their differences well, are sensitive." We do know very well when the meeting is not structured well and when people do not behave well interpersonally.

My business, when I am a facilitator of a meeting, is to provide a process that moves the task towards conclusion. I remember being told by a pastor and group leader who had asked me to help them that I should expect a lot of anger and hostility at this meeting. With the help of some newsprint and magic markers and the structure I am about to propose to you, we moved along well, there was no hostility and people were quite civilized with each other, even in their disagreements.

Edgar de Bono, the noted expert on brain functioning tells us "that left to ourselves our brains are designed to be brilliantly uncreative." Brains are designed to form their own patterns and then to use those patterns on every possible occasion in the future. We become "imprisoned in our usual brain sequences." Individuals spontaneously use their past patterning in processing to confront any new question and speak out what occurs to them at the moment. Facilitators need to structure what might be random comments into a process where contributions are made at the appropriate time and the group can move together through issues by doing brain operations one at a time. Facilitators are orchestra conductors calling up instruments as needed. Orchestra members should not just play whatever music they want at any time, even if they are good solo performers.

For example, if a staff or pastoral council is considering what might be done in youth ministry, the discussion often goes something like the following:

1. I think we should hire a youth minister.
2. I wonder what other parishes are doing.
3. I don't think we know what we want to do. What is it that we want to do?
4. It certainly is the most important thing we need to do now in the parish.
5. We once had a great sports program that attracted a lot of kids.
6. I think we need to reconsider our Confirmation program.
7. I liked John's idea about hiring a youth minister.

8. Our youth program is just dead.

9. It's so hard to reach kids today.

10. I have heard of a program called "Lifeteen" that we ought to investigate.

11. Maybe we should contact the diocesan office for Youth Ministry.

Meetings of this sort are a sad example of the beginnings of frustration and energy-drain. We need to do something else.

The structured process I offer you is one that has been through a number of revisions. I first saw something like it in a United Church of Christ planning manual; later Management Design Institute (MDI) developed a modified version; the Center for Ministry Training in the diocese of Paterson modified it further, and I have added a few notes of my own over the last twenty years.

This is an eight-step-planning model. It is not as formidable as it may look at first glance. When I have conducted pastoral council training sessions I ask the participants to imagine situations like planning a vacation, buying an automobile, a couch, and even choosing a marriage partner. All these stages of planning are involved in planning to do anything. However, research indicates that most people have favorite phases of the process and tend to speak to that primarily. Some people are natural visionaries and want to spend time on the hope and dream; others want to get to action planning as soon as possible, others are strong on information gathering and want to make sure they have enough information, others prefer to critique, others to figure out meanings. The secret of moving the group along is to give adequate time to all functions of understanding and to create a process that is systematic and includes all points of view at the correct time in the process.

The graphic below outlines the process. The numbered items are the eight stages. In the center of the graphic I have listed the "seven ways to gather data" that is an extrapolation of stage two. I have also included an outline entitled "Walking through the Planning Process" that I use to describe how to proceed with the group as you use this process. You will notice that I use evaluation (step eight in the model) as step one when something already exists in parish life that would serve as a starting point for entering into the subject. It is rare to find areas where no previous effort has been made (sexual abuse education and AIDS education have been such areas in recent years).

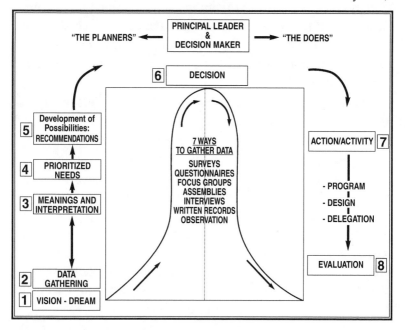

Walking through the Planning Cycle

The description that follows presumes a number of meetings. The number will depend on how large an issue you are discussing. On average, an issue evaluation can be done in 30-40 minutes (if you stick to "listening" and not get into "discussion"). The visioning piece can be done in 30-40 minutes. The data gathering process usually means homework for the group and will take some time. However, the work below (e.g., listing questions to be explored) should take only about 45 minutes.

Step #1 Evaluation of Existing Efforts "what has been"

- Use either a plus-minus list posted on newsprint or a 3-list format (Going Very Well, Going Fairly Well (good enough for now), Needs Improvement).

- The "plus" list or the "Going Very Well" list should be celebrated sometime. It should also be realized that effort is required to keep this "going very well."

- Not much needs to be said of the "Fairly Well list."

- After completing the "minus" list or the "Needs Improvement" list, thematize it. Do this yourself at a break or ask the group to do this with you. There will usually be 4-9 themes and a few individual items that may not fit any theme category.

- I use a formula popularized by Interaction Associates to prioritize the theme list. n/3 is a consensus formula that attempts to see how close we are to agreement without discussion. In n/3 each person is given a number of votes corresponding to 1/3 of the items on the list, e.g., if there are 6 items, each person is given two votes. When the votes are tallied, the highest scored items are the themes the group believes most important.

- You will have finished the evaluation piece with a list of priority areas needing improvement. Just keep this in sight of the group as you go to Step #2.

Step #2 Visioning "like it to be"

- Newsprint a visioning list by asking the group to imagine 3 years from now and describe outcomes they hope for in the area we are considering. The focus question is: "What would it look like if we succeeded?" It is important to make sure this list be of observable behavior.

- After everyone has had an opportunity to give their vision items, I would again use n/3 to prioritize this list.

- Keep this list in sight of the group as you go to Step #3.

Step #3 Data Gathering "what we need to know" "who we need to consult"

- Ask the group to answer the question: "What do we need to know?" Now have the group make a list of questions that they need to explore.

- Usually there are a good number of questions. Write them up as given and when finished use n/3 to determine what the group sees as the most important ones.

- The group may need to explore many or most of the questions but it is important to do very good data gathering on the higher priority questions.

- Then make a list of "who we need to consult" about these questions.

- Individual members or small groups then assume responsibility for working on these questions during the following weeks. A report should be given to the group in the following meetings as data gathering is completed.

Step # 4 Interpretation of Data "what this means"

- The group now responds to the question: "What this data seems to mean to us?" Have the group make a preliminary summary of themes. Some individual or small groups may need to refine and summarize.

Step #5 Prioritizing "most important is"

- At this point the interpretation needs prioritization (i.e., the major learnings from this data are . . . , of slightly less importance is . . . , etc.)

Step #6 Recommendations "would be best to do"

- The group is ready to say: "We recommend that the following be done."

Step # 7-8 Decision and Implementation "will do" "who, what, when"

- Now the group or whoever has decision-making power has to say a final "yes" to the recommendations and set up the machinery for implementation.

Planning done by a parish staff for a Lenten or Advent program using this model could take about 2-3 hours over a few meetings. Planning by a pastoral council about a youth ministry group program might take six or nine months depending on whether you are developing a comprehensive youth program or creating part of a program, like a retreat or peer group counseling program.

In any case, I encourage you to be systematic in what you do. Following such a process as I describe might seem awkward or artificial (the first two stages of learning a new skill) to you. It will feel like work. I assure you it will be better than anything else you have done in working together.

Appendix 1

Self-Managed Teams in Parishes

I WORK as a consultant to parishes that want to do better at what they are doing. I am usually asked to advise parishes that are very busy with programs and concerned about developing ministries among the laity. Staffs in such parishes are concerned about the empowerment of laity and tend to be ready to think in new ways.

On the back cover of a recent issue of the *Journal of the American Society for Training Development,* an advertisement from Zenger Miller (a personnel development company) contained the table reproduced on the next page. I recognized it immediately as a description of what I think is needed to understand how parishes should move to be effective today.

Column 1 of the table can easily be seen as the pre-Vatican paradigm for local church leadership. Column 2 looks very like the church that Vatican II promoted in its documents. Column 3 definitely seems to me to be the kind of church we need to build at the local level today. It is time now to move beyond involving people in ministries to building parish ministries into self-managed teams or communities. The key concept in such a shift is to believe that we can find people mature enough to plan, manage, and evaluate their performance without outside supervision by pastor or staff. Don't get nervous yet—this process will actively involve pastor and staff in selection and training during the early stages. The vision I offer is one in which the right people are in the right ministries; they are formed to do those ministries well, and they are trusted to perform well.

LEADERSHIP

Activities Found in a Traditional Workplace	Skills Required in a More Participative Workplace	Additional Skills Required in a Team Environment
Direct people	Involve people	Inspire teamwork
Explain decisions	Get input for decisions	Facilitate and support decisions
Train individuals	Develop individual performance	Expand team capabilities
Contain conflict	Resolve conflict	Leverage team differences
React to change	Initiate change	Champion innovation
Manage one to one	Coordinate the group	Create team identity and responsibility

Reprinted by permission. Copyright Zenger Miller.

New Roles Necessary

My first experience of the self-managed team was in a parish in Oklahoma, where I saw a group of eighty young married couples who met monthly. The group was entirely in charge of its own meetings and program. Staff members were welcome at meetings but not responsible for the program. Patrick Brennan describes this kind of situation when he says, "I will not begin a ministry without developing lay leaders and a ministering team that will own the ministry."

With self-managed teams, pastor and staff serve as educators and resource people, not as coordinators and supervisors. All over the developed world today, this formula is being tested. For the first time in American history, reorganization has come to mean letting go of middle managers, creating teams, building competency and trust, and lowering supervision. In the book *Leading Teams*, John Zenger describes the condition that creates malaise in organizations: "Stuck organizations are management-centered . . . [managers] see themselves as the central players in the organization and assume they need to control everything." Peter Block is right when he says in *Stewardship* that clarity of requirements, not control, is what is important in today's environment.

It is interesting to observe that for some years now, both bereavement groups and groups of divorced and separated Catholics have been largely self-managed. In most parishes these groups ask for a meeting room and then take care of their own program. Usually, a diocesan office of family life arranges for group leader training. The enthusiasm is there, and adequate training is provided. There is no apparent need for parish staff management.

The Saint Vincent de Paul Society and the Legion of Mary have always been most cooperative with pastors and staffs but have always been largely independent of local staff supervision. Much of this may be due to a strong diocesan, national, or international structure. The people at the local level have known how to take guidelines and do ministry for themselves. The point is that parishes already have self-managed ministries in a number of places. We now need to extend the practice in systematic ways to all parish ministry groups.

Rethinking Management

For five major reasons, now is the time to get serious about rethinking our way of managing parish ministry.

The first reason is that God is doing something in the world. God wants empowered people to use their gifts for the community. People coming to spiritual maturity in the parish have management gifts in ministry. The less they are blocked from using those gifts, the more those gifts can develop.

Second, many of our parishioners have been involved in group work and skill training in their workplaces. Their familiarity with team training, skill development, and systematic planning is abundantly evident when they participate in my workshops on collaborative skills.

Third, the concept of "gifts," which we have used since Vatican II, has caught up with us. Many of our core parishioners believe it, and they want to be more responsible now. As Max De Pree says of American workers in his book *Leadership Jazz*, "The great majority are well-prepared and thoroughly motivated. They need participatory structures." De Pree feels so strongly about using the gifts of people that he calls thwarting human potential a betrayal. The major sin of those in authority is preventing the use of gifts by people.

Fourth, we will never accomplish all the things we need to do in parishes if we don't find new ways of working. I like to ask parish staffs to make lists of all the things they would like to do if they had the time. I have never gotten a list of fewer than twenty items. We may never get to full-scale evangelization if all we do is maintain what we are doing and do that with shrinking resources.

Fifth, there is the distinction made by Peter Block about the need to move American institutions toward stewardship. He sees so many American institutions struggling with patriarchy and its cousin, parenting. The call to stewardship is a call to partnership. Dependency is characteristic of both patriarchal and parental approaches to organizing. If I am to "own" my local church, I need to become a partner in it today. Patriarchy and parenting may have been necessary for sociological reasons at other times, but they won't work in present-day America. Block leaves us with what he calls the two most useful questions he knows for organizations today: (1) How would partners handle this? (2) What policy or structure would we create if this were a partnership?

In the 1990s some new archetypes of leaders and managers have been emerging. The leader is not just the visionary, charismatic, creative, prophetic one. The manager is not just the persevering, systematic, rational, pragmatic one. The first time I noticed an indication of a change in those ideas was about eight years ago, when the American Management Association offered a five-day workshop entitled "Coaching and Counseling Skills for Managers." Today's leaders and managers are being asked to work more collaboratively, with a team orientation. The commitment is clear in secular America. I always think back to the first chapter of Acts and note that the church invented this gift-based community experience. It is time to reclaim our birthright. The new archetypes for pastors and staffs have much more to do with educating and mentoring than with control and supervision.

Developing Self-Managed Teams

In an article in *Church* magazine, Matthias Neumann, writing about collaborative ministry, observed that "we need to commit to ongoing education. . . . It ought to be taken for granted that team ministry will challenge us to learn and interiorize new social skills." Stephen Covey, in *The Seven Habits of Highly Effective People*, tells us that collaborative ministry will require "openness, a spirit of adventure, a high tolerance of ambiguity, low structure certainty and [lack of] predictability." I believe that attaining these qualities is within the range of average people, especially once they know they are expected to do so.

Having digested much of what has been written about self-managed teams, and having been a practitioner in a number of good parishes, I have come to the conclusion that there are five characteristics of good team development within staffs or ministerial groups.

Group vision is crucial and must be arrived at by the exploration of individual members' visions and priorities. The group must discuss such questions as, Why are you here? What do you hope for? What keeps you going and gives you life? What do you think is most important for us to accomplish? In doing so, the members must share at a deep level that will bind them together. Common elements in individuals' responses should then be summarized in an expression of the group's vision. No more than simple facilitator training is necessary to guide this process. Peter Senge's book *The Fifth Discipline* has an excellent chapter on shared vision.

Mutual accountability assumes that everything that is going on belongs to everyone. In terms of parish staff responsibility, this means that although someone may be the "primary responsible" person, everyone in the group is responsible for success. As John Zenger says, "stuck organizations . . . see themselves primarily as... collection[s] of separate departments . . . as silos of vertical power." The sense that everyone is responsible for thinking about everything can foster tremendous energy in a group. Of course, sensitivity regarding ministerial turf must be tempered if others are also responsible in an area for which one is the primary responsible member.

Synergy is the effect of a process that engages people who accept mutual accountability. Stephen Covey makes the case for exciting organizations. As he notes, everything in the natural world is synergistic. All one's bodily organs are interrelated; all one's brain parts are made to work together; all plant life needs the rest of nature—earth, air, water, and fire (plants even commingle roots, and increased richness results). Married people are highly synergistic with their spouses; families can't escape synergy. For Covey, the world of human relationships is the most catalytic, unifying, and exciting of all the synergies: "The more genuine the involvement, the more sincere and sustained the participation in analyzing and solving problems, the greater the release of everyone's creativity and of the commitment to what they create. This, I'm convinced, is the essence of power in the Japanese approach to business, which has changed the world marketplace." Perhaps you have attended some good meetings and noticed that all sorts of new alternatives begin to open up through personal interaction. Some companies today have departments of innovation, whose major task is not to come up with new ideas but to create new ways of thinking that can help other departments become creative with their own members. Groups usually need help in learning to structure synergy.

Group decision making comes naturally to a mutually accountable group operating in a synergistic way. The right people are assembled, and they are responsible and creative as a group. They can be trusted. The role of the pastor in such a meeting is to support and facilitate decisions. Why wouldn't he? This is a highly functioning group, and an idea will get a wealth of testing. If this seems unrealistic to you, remember that I am describing the work of a team after much development has taken place. That development can be structured, as I will discuss later.

Support is a natural outcome of the preceding processes. People become more interdependent by working in an environment of common vision, mutual accountability, synergy, and group decision making. It is important to recognize what Jon R. Katzenbach and Douglas Smith observe in *The Wisdom of Teams:* "The emphasis is on the challenge of the task, not team-promoting enterprises. . . . Teams founder without a performance challenge." Members' support for one another will be a by-product of their working together well.

Writers about the team approach tell us that excellent teams are rare. When I visit a parish that wants to develop self-managed teams, I ask the staff to assess existing ministries and put them into one of the following categories: Presently self-managed / Close to self-management / Could be ready within two years / Could be ready with new leadership / Far from ready / Will never be ready. It is not hard for a staff to do this kind of categorizing.

Next comes the planning of a strategy for moving ministry teams to assume more responsibility for themselves. The key to developing and moving groups is found in the "situational leadership" model, made popular by Ken Blanchard, who recently wrote a book entitled *The One-Minute Manager Builds High-Performing Teams*. In Blanchard's model, four leader behaviors may be called for, depending on the maturity level of the individual or group: directing, coaching, supporting, and delegating. As in all situational leadership theories, the leader has to assess the group's degree of maturity and use those behaviors in trying to move the group toward full maturity. The first stage, directing, includes setting forth visions and goals, providing training in skills, and clarifying roles. In the first stage, it is the leader who is primarily responsible for setting direction. In stage two, coaching, the group needs help with its situation, and the leader needs to be sensitive to how the group is getting stuck and what resources might be helpful. In stage three, supporting, the group has moved toward more maturity and knowledge and can do most things for itself. The members have become partners. They may still need to discuss some things with leaders, but now do so as equals. The need for additional skills may emerge in team members' self-evaluations. Leaders may serve as resources or provide referrals at this stage.

In the fourth stage, delegating, groups can operate independently and can be trusted to do their tasks well. They have arrived at a healthy independence and can meet their own needs, including the need for recognition of a ministry well performed. They have become responsible for their own direction and support. If they haven't managed the task

of interdependence with other ministries, it is the creative task of the leader to provoke the group's attention to that issue.

As I conclude this overview of self-managed team ministry, I am reminded of Stephen Covey's remark on why people don't change their way of working when they know that things are not quite right: (1) they are not hurting enough; and (2) they don't want to change their lifestyle. That gives us cause to pause and reflect.

The journey is exciting. The pastors and staffs that have embarked on it are the most energized people I know. It took God six days to create. It may be just day one or two for us, but the early days of creation are very important.

Recommended Reading

Belbin, M. *Management Teams*. San Diego, California: Pfeiffer, 1994.

Block, P. *Stewardship*. San Francisco, California: Berrett-Koehler, 1993.

De Pree, M. *Leadership as an Art*. New York, New York: Doubleday, 1989.

De Pree, M. *Leadership Jazz*. New York, New York: Doubleday, 1992.

Katzenbach, J., and O. Smith. *The Wisdom of Teams*. Boston, Massachusetts: Harvard Business School Press, 1993.

Zenger, J., E. Musselwhite, K. Hurson, and C. Perrin. *Leading Teams*. Homewood, Illinois: Business One Irwin, 1994.

This essay by Joseph Lynch, SM appeared in *Human Development*, Volume 17, Number 3, Fall 1996, pp. 16-19. *Human Development* can be obtained by writing directly to: HUMAN DEVELOPMENT, P.O. Box 3000, Dept. HD, Denville, NJ 07834.

Prayer Resources

Use one of the following readings or prayers to open the meeting (each person should have a copy).
Allow a few moments for silent reflection followed by sharing.

Readings for Reflection

Trust in the Lord of the Journey

Above all, trust in the slow work of God.
  impatient in everything
  to reach the end without delay.

We should like to skip
  the intermediate stages;
we are impatient of being on the way
  to something unknown,
  something new.
And yet, it is the law of all progress
  that it is made by passing through
  some stages of instability . . .
  and that may take a very long time.
And so, I think it is with you,
  your ideas mature gradually—
  let them grow.
Let them shape themselves,
  without undue haste.
Don't try to force them on,
  as though you could be today
  what time (that is to say, grace and
  circumstances acting on your own good will)
  will make you tomorrow.
Only God could say what this new spirit
  gradually forming within you will be.

Give our Lord the benefit of believing
    that His Hand is leading you,
    and accept the anxiety of
    feeling yourself in suspense and incomplete.
                            —Pierre Teilhard de Chardin

Our vocation is not simply to be—but to work together
with God in the creation of our own life, our own identity, our
own destiny. We are free beings and children of God. This
means to say that we should not passively exist but actively
participate in His creative freedom in our own lives and the
lives of others by choosing truth.   —Thomas Merton

It helps, now and then, to step back
and take the long view.
The kingdom is not only beyond our efforts,
it is even beyond our vision.

We accomplish in our lifestyle only a fraction of
the magnificent enterprise that is God's work.
Nothing we do is complete,
which is another way of saying
that the kingdom always lies beyond us.

No statement says all that could be said.
No prayer fully expresses our faith.
No confession brings perfection.
No pastoral visit brings wholeness.
No program accomplishes the Church's mission.
No set of goals and objectives includes everything.

This is what we are about.
We plant the seeds that one day will grow.
We water seeds already planted,
Knowing that they hold future promise.

We lay foundations that will need further development.
We provide yeast that produces effects far beyond
our capabilities.

We cannot do everything,
and there is a sense of liberation in that.
This enables us to do something,
and to do it very well.
It may be incomplete, but it is a beginning, a step along the way,
an opportunity for the Lord's grace to enter and do the rest.

We may never see the results,
but that is the difference between the master builder and
the worker.
We are the workers, not master builders,
ministers, not messiahs.
We are prophets of a future not our own.

—ARCHBISHOP OSCAR ROMERO

The pope said that for all Christians "the school of faith is not a triumphal march, but a journey peppered with suffering and love," trials and a faithfulness that needs to be renewed every day.

When Jesus asked St. Peter three times: "Do you love me?" St. Peter replied yes, but he felt his love was inadequate, limited by his human heart and doubts, the pope said.

But slowly St. Peter realized that his impoverished love was enough for Jesus, because "Jesus adapts himself to Peter, not Peter to Jesus," the pope said.

Pope Benedict said Jesus works around people's weaknesses. The faithful follow Christ with their limited capacity to love and remain open to his will because "we know Jesus is good and that he accepts us," he said. Because Jesus accepted St. Peter's fragile love and told him to follow, St. Peter's journey of faith was marked by hope, the pope said, because he knew the Lord was always with him.

Peter and all Christians become steadfast witnesses not by becoming perfect, but by remaining "constantly open to the work of the Spirit," he said.

—POPE BENEDICT XVI
Catholic Trends, May 2006

The thoughts I would have at the hour of death (and which I have now): to realize that I am going to discover the affectionate God. It is impossible that God should deceive me, the very idea is monstrous! I will go to Him and say: I can do nothing except trust in Your goodness. In this lies my strength, yes, all my strength.

If this leaves me, if this confidence in Love deserts me, I should be finished, because I have no belief worth anything supernaturally, whatever that may mean; and if one has to be worthy of blessing in order to have it, that is the way to lose it. But the further I go, the clearer I see that I have good reason for picturing my Father as Infinite Kindness.

And let the masters of the spiritual life say what they will, let them speak of justice, exigencies, dread, or judgment; I believe my judge to be One Who goes up the watch-tower every day and scans the horizon to see whether His prodigal son is returning to Him. Who would not want to be judged by Him? St. John has written: "Love is not yet perfect in one who is afraid." I have no fear of God, but this is not so much because I love Him as that I know I am loved by Him.

And I find no need to ask myself why my Father loves me, or what He loves in me. Besides, I should find it a very embarrassing question to answer; indeed it is one that is really impossible to answer. He loves me because He is Love, and I have only to accept this fact for it to become effective. But it is necessary to make this voluntary gesture of acceptance. This is the intrinsic beauty of willing love. Love does not impose Himself: He offers Himself.

O my Father, thank You for loving me! And I shall not be one to cry out that I am unworthy! In any case, to love me, such a one as I am, this is indeed worthy of You, worthy of essential Love, worthy of essentially gratuitous love! How enchanting this thought is for me! Herein lies my refuge from scruples, from discouraging false humility, and from sadness of spirit.

We are apt to think too much of ourselves and not enough of God. There are some unfortunate theologians who are afraid of making God too good (though they are unaware of it)—that is to say, too beautiful. "He is good but He is not weak," they say. But a goodness, or bounty, that will not go as far as a kind of weakness (or rather, what we in our hardness call weakness) is that kind of bounty which is afraid of encouraging beggars to be lazy, and restricts its giving.

Weak through love, my Father is so much the greater and more beautiful. The Cross shows me this.

—AUGUSTE VALENSIN

We drove into town with Senator Dawson, a neighbor of the monastery, and all the while I wondered how I would react at meeting once again, face to face, the wicked world. I met the world and I found it no longer so wicked after all. Perhaps the things I had resented about the world when I left it were defects of my own that I had projected upon it. Now on the contrary, I found that everything stirred me with a deep and mute sense of compassion. Perhaps some of the people we saw going about the streets were hard and tough. . . . but I did not stop to observe it because I seemed to have lost an eye for merely exterior detail and to have discovered, instead, a deep sense of respect and love and pity for the souls that such details never fully reveal. I went through the city, realizing for the first time in my life how good are all the people in the world and how much value they have in the sight of God!

—THOMAS MERTON

This toy . . . intrigued me, and for a long time I kept wondering just what could produce so delightful a phenomenon. One day a careful examination revealed that the unusual effect was merely the result of a combination of tiny scraps of paper and wool scattered about inside. When on further scrutiny I discovered three looking-glasses inside the tube, the puzzle was solved. And this simple toy became for me the image of a great mystery. . . . So long as our actions, even the most trivial, remain within love's kaleidoscope, the Blessed Trinity (which the three converging glasses represent) imparts to them a marvellous brightness and beauty. . . . The eye-piece of the spyglass symbolizes the good God, who looking from the outside (but through Himself, as it were) into the kaleidoscope finds everything quite beautiful, even our miserable straws of effort and our most insignificant actions.

—THERESE OF LISIEUX

Closing Prayers

Use one of the following prayers to end a meeting. Each person should have a copy to pray together at the meeting and to take home for continued thought and prayer until the next gathering.

Take, Lord, Receive

Take, Lord, and receive all my liberty,
my memory, my understanding, and my entire will.,
all that I have and call my own.
You have given it all to me.
To you, Lord, I return it.
Everything is yours;
do with it what you will.
Give me only your love and your grace.
That is enough for me.   —ST. IGNATIUS OF LOYOLA

God Our Father

God our Father,
   We believe that where people are gathered together in love
      You are present and good things happen.
We believe that we are immersed in mystery
   that our lives are more than they seem.
We believe that you are after us
   that you are calling to us from the depth of human life.
We believe that the Spirit of Peace
   is present with us.
And most deeply, we believe that in our striving to love and to
      serve
   we make You present in the world.
Lord guide us in our efforts
   to share the message of your "Good News."
      Lead us to a deeper awareness and love for you.
We ask this in Jesus' name. Amen.

Prayer for All Who Minister in the Church

Lord, I pray for all who witness for you in this world;
ministers, priests, and bishops,
men and women who have dedicated their lives to you,
and all those who try to bring the light of the gospel into the
      darkness of this age.
Give them courage, strength, perseverance, and hope;
fill their hearts and minds
with the knowledge of your presence,
and let them experience your name
as their refuge from all dangers.
Most of all, give them the joy of your Spirit,
so that wherever they go and whomever they meet

they will remove the veil
of depression, fatalism, and defeatism
and will bring new life to the many
who live in constant fear of death.
Lord, be with all who bring the Good News. Amen.

—HENRI NOUWEN

Prayer of St. Francis

Lord, make me an instrument of your peace.
Where there is hatred, let me sow love.
Where there is injury, forgiveness.
Where there are doubts, faith.
Where there is darkness, light.
Where there is sadness, joy.
O divine Master,
grant that I may not so much seek
to be consoled as to console;
to be understood as to understand;
to be loved as to love.
For it is in giving that we receive;
it is in pardoning that we are pardoned;
and it is in dying that we are born to eternal life.   *Traditional*

Blessed Be the Lord

Blessed be the Lord, the creator, the God of the future.
Blessed be Jesus, the one who weaves God's future.
Blessed be his vision, speaking to us of new wineskins.
Blessed be his courage in stepping beyond the familiar.
Blessed be his trust in the desolation of his dying.
Blessed be the Spirit, the outpouring of Jesus' rising,
Making all weary pilgrims new.
Glory be to the Father and to the Son and to the Holy Spirit
As it was in the beginning, is now and ever shall be,
World without end. Amen.

Bibliography

Barber, Benjamin. *Consumed.* New York: W.W. Norton, 2007.
—*Jihad vs McWorld.* New York: Ballantine Books, 1995.

Bennis, Warren. *Leaders.* Cambridge: Harper & Row, 1985.
—*Organizational Genius.* Reading: Addison-Wesley, 1996.
—*Why Leaders Can't Lead.* San Francisco: Jossey-Bass, 1989.

Bly, Robert. *The Sibling Society.* Reading: Addison-Wesley, 1996.

Boyack, Kenneth ed. *The New Evangelization.* Mahwah: Paulist Press, 1992.

Brennan, Patrick. *The Evangelizing Parish.* Allen: Tabor Publishing, 1987.
—*The Mission Driven Parish.* Maryknoll: Orbis Books, 2007.
—*Re-Imagining Evangelization.* New York: Crossroad Publishing, 1995.
—*Re-Imagining the Parish.* New York: Crossroad Publishing, 1991.

Brueggeman, Walter. *Biblical Perspectives on Evangelization.* Nashville: Abingdon Press, 1993.
—*David's Truth.* Philadelphia: Fortress Press, 1985.
—*Hopeful Imagination.* Philadelphia: Fortress Press, 1986.
—*The Prophetic Imagination.* Philadelphia: Fortress Press, 1978.

Bugbee, Bruce. *What You Do Best In the Body of Christ.* Grand Rapids: Zondervan,1995.
—*Network: The Right People . . . In the Right Places . . . For the Right Reasons.* Grand Rapids: Zondervan, 1994.

Champlin, Joseph. *The Marginal Catholic.* Notre Dame: Ave Maria Press, 1989.

Desiano, Frank. *Creating the Evangelizing Parish.* Mahwah: Paulist Press, 1993.
—*Sowing New Seed.* Mahwah: Paulist Press, 1994.

Donnelly, Doris ed. *Retrieving Charisms For the Twenty First Century.* Collegeville: The Liturgical Press, 1999.

Downey, Michael. *Understanding Christian Spirituality*. Mahwah: Paulist Press, 1997.

Ewen, Scott. *All Consuming Images*. New York: Harper Collins, 1988.

—*Captains of Consciousness*. Minneapolis: University of Minnesota Press, 1992.

—*Channels of Desire*. Minneapolis: University of Minnesota Press, 1992.

Fichter, Joseph. *Dynamics of a City Church*. Chicago: University of Chicago Press, 1951.

—*Social Relations in the Urban Parish*. Chicago: University of Chicago Press, 1954.

—*Southern Parish*. Chicago: University of Chicago Press, 1951.

Fore, William F. Mythmakers: *Gospel, Culture and the Media*. New York: Friendship Press, 1990.

Gallagher S.J. Michael Paul. *Can I Be a Christian On My Own?* London: Darton, Longman & Todd, 1991.

—*Clashing Symbols*. Mahwah: Paulist Press, 1998.

—*Free to Believe*. Chicago: Loyola University Press, 1987.

—*Help My Unbelief*. Chicago: Loyola University Press, 1988.

—*The Human Poetry of Faith*. Mahwah: Paulist Press, 2001.

—*Letters on Prayer*. London: Darton, Longman & Todd, 1994.

—*Struggles of Faith*. London: Columba Press, 1990.

—*What Are They Saying About Faith?* Mahwah: Paulist Press, 1995.

—*What Will Give Us Happiness?* Dublin: Veritas Publications, 1992.

—*Where Is Your God*. London: Darton, Longman & Todd, 1991.

—*Will Our Children Believe?* Dublin: Veritas Publications, 1998.

Gitlin, Todd ed. *Watching Television*. New York: Pantheon, 1987.

Gleick, James. *Faster.* New York: Pantheon, 1999.

Haring, Bernard. *My Hope for the Church.* Ligouri: Ligouri Press, 1999.

Haughey, John. *Re-Visiting the Idea of Vocation.* Washington: Catholic University Press, 2004.

Hicks, Dr. Rick & Kathy. *Boomers, X-ers, and Other Strangers.* Wheaton: Tyndale House, 1999.

Hine, Thomas. *I Want That.* New York: Harper Collins, 2002.

Howe, Neil & Strauss William. *The Fourth Turning.* New York: Bantam Doubleday, 1997.
—*Generations.* New York: William Morrow, 1991.
—*Millenials Rising.* New York: Vintage Books, 2000.

Hunter, George. *Church for the Un-Churched.* Nashville: Abingdon Press, 1996.
—*How to Reach Secular People.* Nashville: Abingdon Press, 1992.

Hybels, Lynne & Bill. *Re-Discovering Church.* Grand Rapids: Zondervan Publishing House, 1995.

Jhally Sut. *The Codes of Advertising.* New York: Routledge, 1987.

Kasser, Tim. *The High Price of Materialism.* Cambridge: MIT Press, 2002.

Kavanaugh, John Francis. *Following Christ in a Consumer Society.* Maryknoll: Orbis Books, 1982.

Kennedy, Eugene. *Tomorrow's Catholics, Yesterday's Church.* New York: Harper& Row, 1988.

Lasch, Christopher. *The Culture of Narcissism.* New York: W.W. Norton, 1979.
—*The True and Only Heaven.* New York: W.W. Norton, 1991.

Mead, Loren. *The Once and Future Church: Re-Inventing The Congregation.* Washington, D.C.: Alban Institute, 1991.

Meagher, John C. *The Truing of Christianity.* New York: Doubleday, 1990.

Meyrowitz, Joshua. *No Sense of Place.* New York: Oxford University Press, 1985.

Miller, Vincent J. *Consuming Religion.* New York: Continuum Publishing Group, 2004.

Mumford, Lewis. *The Condition of Man.* New York: Harcourt Brace Jovanovich, 1944.

Neafsey, John. *A Sacred Voice Is Calling.* Maryknoll: Orbis Books, 2006.

Postman, Neil. *Amusing Ourselves to Death.* New York: Penguin Books, 1985.
—*The Disappearance of Childhood.* New York: Vintage Books, 1982.

Rahner, Karl. *Belief Today.* London: Sheed & Ward, 1973
—*Concern for the Church.* New York: Crossroad, 1986.
—*Opportunities for Faith.* New York: Seabury, 1974.

Rolheiser, Ronald. *Secularity and the Gospel.* New York: Crossroad, 2006.

Roof, Wade Clark. *A Generation of Seekers.* San Francisco: Harper Collins, 1993.
—*Spiritual Marketplace.* Princeton: Princeton University Press, 1999.

Ruggiero, Vincent Ryan. *Nonsense Is Destroying America.* Nashville: Thomas Nelson, 1994.

Schaller, Lyle. *The Very Large Church.* Nashville: Abingdon Press, 2000.
—*The Middle Size Church.* Nashville: Abingdon Press, 1985.
—*The Multiple Staff and the Larger Church.* Nashville: Abingdon Press, 1980.

Schorr, Juliet. *Born to Buy.* New York: Scribner, 2004.
—*The Overspent American.* New York: Basic Books, 1998
—*The Overworked American.* New York: Basic Books, 1991.

Schultze, Quentin ed. *Dancing in the Dark.* Grand Rapids: Eerdmans, 1991.

—*Redeeming Television.* Downers Grove: Intervarsity Press, 1992.

—*Winning Your Kids Back from the Media.* Downers Grove: Intervarsity Press, 1994.

Taylor, Charles. *A Catholic Modernity.* New York: Oxford University Press, 1999.

—*The Ethics of Authenticity.* Cambridge: Harvard University Press, 1991.

—*A Secular Age.* Cambridge: Harvard University Press, 2007.

—*Sources of the Self.* Cambridge: Harvard University Press, 1989.

Trow, George. *In the Context of No Context.* Boston: Little Brown & Co., 1981.

Wachtel, Paul. *The Poverty of Affluence.* Philadelphia: New Society Publishers, 1989.

Warren, Michael. *Communications and Cultural Analysis.* Westport: Bergin & Garvey, 1992.

Weddell, Sherry. *Making Disciples, Equipping Apostles.* Colorodo Springs: Catherine of Siena Institute, 2001.

Whybrow, Peter C. *American Mania.* New York: W.W. Norton, 2005.

Wolf, Naomi. *The Beauty Myth.* New York: Doubleday, 1992.

Wuthnow, Robert. *Christianity in the 21st Century.* New York: Oxford University Press, 1993.

—*Learning to Care.* New York: Oxford University Press, 1995.

Yankelovich, Daniel. "New Rules in American Life: Searching for Self-Fulfillment in a World Turned Upside Down". *Psychology Today,* April, 1961.

Additional Titles Published by Resurrection Press, a Catholic Book Publishing Imprint

A Rachel Rosary *Larry Kupferman*	$4.50
Blessings All Around *Dolores Leckey*	$8.95
Catholic Is Wonderful *Mitch Finley*	$4.95
The Dilemma of Divorced Catholics *John Catoir*	$8.95
Discernment *Chris Aridas*	$8.95
Feasts of Life *Jim Vlaun*	$12.95
Grace Notes *Lorraine Murray*	$9.95
Healing through the Mass *Robert DeGrandis, SSJ*	$9.95
Healing Your Grief *Ruthann Williams, OP*	$7.95
Heart Peace *Adolfo Quezada*	$9.95
How Shall We Become Holy? *Mary Best*	$6.95
How Shall We Celebrate? *Lorraine Murray*	$6.95
How Shall We Pray? *James Gaffney*	$5.95
The Joy of Being an Altar Server *Joseph Champlin*	$5.95
The Joy of Being a Bereavement Minister *Nancy Stout*	$5.95
The Joy of Being a Catechist *Gloria Durka*	$4.95
The Joy of Being a Eucharistic Minister *Mitch Finley*	$5.95
The Joy of Being a Lector *Mitch Finley*	$5.95
The Joy of Being an Usher *Gretchen Hailer, RSHM*	$5.95
The Joy of Marriage Preparation *McDonough/Marinelli*	$5.95
The Joy of Music Ministry *J.M. Talbot*	$6.95
The Joy of Pilgrimage *Lori Erickson*	$6.95
The Joy of Praying the Psalms *Nancy de Flon*	$5.95
The Joy of Praying the Rosary *James McNamara*	$5.95
The Joy of Preaching *Rod Damico*	$6.95
The Joy of Teaching *Joanmarie Smith*	$5.95
The Joy of Worshiping Together *Rod Damico*	$5.95
Lessons for Living from the 23rd Psalm *Victor Parachin*	$6.95
Lights in the Darkness *Ave Clark, O.P.*	$8.95
Loving Yourself for God's Sake *Adolfo Quezada*	$5.95
Magnetized by God *Robert E. Lauder*	$8.95
Meditations for Survivors of Suicide *Joni Woelfel*	$8.95
Mercy Flows *Rod Damico*	$9.95
Mother Teresa *Eugene Palumbo, S.D.B.*	$5.95
Mourning Sickness *Keith Smith*	$8.95
Our Grounds for Hope *Fulton J. Sheen*	$7.95
Personally Speaking *Jim Lisante*	$8.95
Power of One *Jim Lisante*	$9.95
Praying the Lord's Prayer with Mary *Muto/vanKaam*	$8.95
5-Minute Miracles *Linda Schubert*	$4.95
Sabbath Moments *Adolfo Quezada*	$6.95
Season of New Beginnings *Mitch Finley*	$4.95
Sometimes I Haven't Got a Prayer *Mary Sherry*	$8.95
St. Katharine Drexel *Daniel McSheffery*	$12.95
What He Did for Love *Francis X. Gaeta*	$5.95
Woman Soul *Pat Duffy, OP*	$7.95
You Are My Beloved *Mitch Finley*	$10.95

For a free catalog call 1-800-892-6657
www.catholicbookpublishing.com